"Brian Ashcraft has done us drinkers a real service here. A guide to where Japanese whisky came from and who's making it now, [...] ttles we might want to seek out, it is a reference [...] ith *Japanese Whisky* in hand, I'm off to the liquo[...]"
—Adam Rogers, Deputy Editor *Wired Magazi*[...] *f Booze*

"A tour de force. *Japanese Whisky: The Ultimate Guide to the World's Most Desirable Spirit* combines engrossing and well-researched history with trustworthy tasting notes, fascinating distillery guides and beautiful photography. It's not only an excellent practical look at one of the world's most exciting alcohol traditions but also a great read."
—Chris Bunting, author *Drinking Japan* and founder of *Nonjatta.com*

"*Japanese Whisky: The Ultimate Guide to the World's Most Desirable Spirit* gives deep insight into the spirit's history and also throughly explains the specialties of the drink."
—Horst Luening, *Whisky.com*

"This book's love of the 'water of life' shines through on every page. From the exhaustive account of Japan's long relationship with whisky to the detailed descriptions of labels produced by its world-beating distilleries, *Japanese Whisky* should appeal to experienced buyers and novices alike. The perfect accompaniment to a Japanese single malt."
—Justin McCurry, Tokyo correspondent for the *Guardian*

Japanese whisky has been around for under a century but is now winning all the major international awards. How did this happen and what are the secrets of Japanese whisky makers?

This book features previously unpublished archival images and interviews chronicling the forgotten stories of Japan's pioneering whisky makers. It explains the special materials and methods used by Japanese distillers, including *mizunara* wood, Japanese barley and unique Japanese production methods. It also examines the close cultural connections between Japanese whisky drinkers and their favorite tipples. For the first time in English, over a hundred independently scored reviews are presented from leading Japanese whisky blogger Yuji Kawasaki, which shed new light on Japan's most famous single malts as well as its grain whiskies and blends.

JAPANESE WHISKY

The Ultimate Guide to the World's Most Desirable Spirit

BRIAN ASHCRAFT
WITH IDZUHIKO UEDA AND YUJI KAWASAKI
FOREWORD BY LEW BRYSON

TUTTLE Publishing

Tokyo | Rutland, Vermont | Singapore

ABOUT THIS BOOK

To fully appreciate Japanese whisky, it's necessary to put it in a larger context. For well over 1,500 years Japan has imported language, religion and culture, stamping its own distinct mark on all three. The country takes what it wants or needs and then artfully improves and localizes imports to suit local tastes. This is exactly what happened with whisky. But how? And why? The first part of this book examines how Japanese history, culture and religion have influenced Japanese whisky. The second part delves into the best Japanese whisky makers of today, showing why their stuff is unique and providing reviews and scores of various whiskies so that readers can get a good idea of what to expect from current and future releases. The last chapter introduces some of Japan's newest distilleries and discusses future trends. Note that this is an independent work. None of the authors have ever worked or done consulting for any Japanese whisky maker and all of the whiskies reviewed and scored were paid for out of pocket.

contents

How Did Japanese Whisky Become So Good?

Foreword by Lew Bryson

Up until about 2015, people still asked me pretty frequently, is there really Japanese whisky? After being assured that there most certainly was, the next question was, inevitably, is it any good?

The answer is a most definite yes. Despite the relative youth of Japan's whisky industry and the small number of distillers, the quality and the distinctiveness of the spirits cannot be denied. It is not just good whisky, it is excellent whisky, and some expressions are rightly ranked among the very best in the world.

How did Japanese whisky get to be so good and how did it remain an unknown quantity for so long? As with so many other situations in whisky's evolution, it's all about Scotch. As Japan came out of centuries of isolation in the mid to late 1800s, the ruling classes embraced the West, especially the West's great naval power, the British Empire. Increasingly, that meant drinking Scotch whisky.

By the early 1920s an enterprising Japanese drinks magnate, Shinjiro Torii, realized that there might be money to be made by making whisky in Japan rather than shipping it halfway around the globe. As it happened, a young Japanese chemist, Masataka Taketsuru, had studied whisky making in Scotland and knew what was necessary to make whisky in Japan.

Torii ran the company, which is now known as Suntory, and Taketsuru managed the distillery. Differences arose, which led to friction, and Taketsuru went his own way, founding Nikka and building his own distillery. Each company would later build another malt whisky distillery, and a number of other distillers would follow them, albeit on a much smaller scale.

Japanese whisky thrived, but the other, more established whisky regions, particularly Scotland, had such a head start that Japan's spirit couldn't make any headway. For all practical purposes, if you wanted to drink Japanese whisky, you had to go to Japan.

I was lucky enough to be present at one of the breakthrough moments that changed this state of affairs. As the managing editor of what was then *Malt Advocate* magazine, I was at WhiskyFest Chicago in 2005 when a very hesitant group of Suntory representatives stood behind a table stocking bottles of Yamazaki whisky.

No one knew how things would go but I'd wandered over before the show opened to sample this new exhibitor's whisky. I'd never had Japanese whisky at this point. I asked for a sample of the 18 year old. My mouth fell open. This was great stuff! The component flavors were in balance, the essence of the malt was clear, the wood was not overpowering. I smiled and thanked them for the sample ... and then proceeded to tell everyone who asked what I recommended to "try the Yamazaki."

I must not have been the only one spreading the word. By the end of the show, the Suntory group stood behind an empty table, stunned and smiling. They'd been mobbed by the crowd, who enthusiastically embraced their product. I stopped by and congratulated them and they smiled and bowed and thanked me—for what, I'm not sure! Given the influence of the caliber of the attendees at WhiskyFest—retailers, whisky bar owners and the influential whisky consumers—Yamazaki, and all of Japanese whisky with it, was on the map in America.

People in the know jumped on Japanese whisky. It was excellent and it was largely unknown, and it was, for a brief time, bargain priced. I featured it regularly in tasting events. It was a happy time.

Reality caught up as demand rapidly depleted the stock of long-aged whisky. Japanese distillers were behind the curve, and while distilling can be stepped up, aging whisky takes time that simply can't be rushed. We're living with the consequences of that—much higher prices on harder to find whisky.

It's a whisky market where you need a guide. Congratulations, you have found one! Brian Ashcraft's guide to Japanese whisky takes you into the kind of detail you need to make real buying decisions. What does the whisky taste like, who actually makes it, how is it made? It's all here, in an engaging, well-organized guide.

Japanese whisky, and the whiskey industry worldwide, was taken by surprise by the huge surge in demand over the past fifteen years. Things will get better and we should see more supply. In the meantime, read up, make smart choices and enjoy!

Lew Bryson is the author of Tasting Whiskey: An Insider's Guide to the Unique Pleasures of the World's Finest Spirits

PART ONE

Japanese Whisky Comes of Age

The worldwide fanfare might be recent but Japan has been making whisky for nearly a century. The Japanese have been drinking it even longer than that. Proper whisky making began in 1924 after the country's first legitimate venture, the Yamazaki Distillery, was established a year earlier. The real whisky-making process only became known after a young chemist named Masataka Taketsuru went to Scotland in 1918 to learn first hand how it was done.

The Scots might have showed Japan the way but it was the Americans who introduced the drink when, in July 1853, US naval vessels showed up in Tokyo Bay to force open the country after its more than 200-year period of self-imposed isolation. Americans brought casks of the stuff as well as other presents to show off Yankee know-how, such as a miniature steam train, an early camera and the telegraph. Over the course of the following century, Japan would master all of these, producing world-class trains, cameras and communication systems. Now, Japanese whisky is considered one of the world's original five classic whiskies, joining the likes of Scotch, Irish, Canadian and American.

Throughout the 20th century, Japanese whisky didn't get the respect it deserved but now that's changed. Between 2001 and 2017 Suntory's and Nikka's whiskies have each won over a hundred accolades from the industry's most prestigious international competitions, while other domestic makers such as Venture Whisky, Mars Whisky and the Kirin Distillery have also garnered prizes and international acclaim. Japanese whiskies are hailed as among the world's best. The country's distillers and blenders have also been awarded for their excellence.

It wasn't only awards that Japanese whisky was accumulating. After a steady decline since the 1980s, whisky sales in Japan began increasing in 2008, due in large part to Suntory's highball campaign. Moreover, in 2014 Nikka saw a 124 percent spike in sales thanks to the Japanese TV drama *Massan* about the life of founder Masataka Taketsuru, who also first managed the Yamazaki Distillery. A combination of awards and international attention meant that within a year Nikka was no longer releasing whiskies from its Yoichi and Miyagikyo distilleries with age statements. There simply wasn't the stock, because 10–15 years prior Japan and the whole world wasn't drinking as much Japanese whisky.

Meaning? It wasn't making as much either. Nikka was forced to revamp its line-up, releasing single malts without age statements. Likewise, Suntory's Yamazaki malts with age statements seemed to temporarily vanish from the stores. There was no way that decades earlier the country's whisky makers could have known they were making the world's most desirable spirit—or even the most expensive one.

Left Suntory released its first Yamazaki single malt in 1984. That same year, Nikka released a single malt from the Nikka Hokkaido Distillery, now called the Yoichi Distillery.
Above Visitors at Suntory Yamazaki can peruse the thousands of samples in its whisky library.

At auctions, rare Japanese whiskies are now fetching staggering prices. In 2015, a set of 54 bottles from the former Hanyu Distillery went for HK$3.8 million (US$486,588), while two years later a bidder shelled out HK$1,298,000 (US$166,207) for a 52-year-old Karuizawa. It's not only the defunct distilleries like Hanyu and Karuizawa that command jaw-dropping prices. In 2016, a single bottle of 50-year-old Yamazaki went for HK$850,000 (US$108,842) at auction, making it also one of the most expensive whiskies ever sold. But it's not just the rare stuff that is pricey! Even the available Japanese single malts and blends without age statements are sold at premium prices, often commanding slightly more than their older Scottish counterparts. But whisky fans all over say they're worth it.

The Japanese whisky business hasn't returned to its early 1980s heyday but is doing better than it has in ages, with

Above Many Japanese bartenders dress in white shirts and ties but not all. Here, at Fukuda Bar in Osaka's Takatsuki, Yutaka Fukuda is decked out in a green Guinness T-shirt. Besides Japanese whiskies, the bar has an eclectic selection of Scotch and bourbon.

sales increasing year by year, thanks to increased interest from abroad and to the quality tipple distilleries make. Japanese consumers, who only a few years ago might have thought whisky was dated, fuddy-duddy and hardly hip, have once again become big whisky drinkers, with single malts, pricey blends and fizzy highball drinks enjoyed at restaurants, bars and homes across the country.

The distilleries featured in this book produce world-class, highly lauded whisky. If quality is measured in praise, then whisky doesn't get much better than what Japanese distilleries are making.

Japanese bars are the best places to drink Japanese whisky. Part of the fun of drinking in Japan is walking into a random bar and seeing what they have.

Japanese whisky as we know it would not have been possible without Suntory and Nikka and the two men who founded them—Shinjiro Torii and Masataka Taketsuru. But Suntory and Nikka aren't the only game in town. In fact, from the mid-1950s to the early 1960s Nikka wasn't even the second biggest selling brand in Japan, coming in third place behind Ocean Whisky (for more on Ocean and the now demolished Karuizawa Distillery, see page 28). That changed around 1965 when Nikka pulled into second place behind Suntory. Today, Kirin, Mars Whisky, White Oak and Venture Whisky each have their own approach and their own history. All produce award-winning, world-class stuff. But Japanese whisky does not stop there because there are also brand-new distilleries breaking ground and beginning to tell their own story. At the time of writing, new whisky distilleries are beginning production. An increasing number of Japanese drinks companies are also including whisky in their production line-up or reviving their whisky production. Over time, expect these new and restarted distilleries to make better and better stuff. Maybe one day they'll even find their spot next to the country's best.

Japan's Biggest and Best Whisky Makers

In Japanese culture, the term *ryuko* (龍虎) means "dragon and tiger" and refers to two great rivals. In terms of Japanese whisky, these are Suntory and Nikka. According to a 2016 estimate from *The Nikkei Business Daily*, Suntory commands 56.3 percent of the whisky market and Nikka takes 27.8 percent, with the rest divvied up among other producers. Some whisky drinkers say they prefer Suntory's products while others say they like Nikka's best. As whisky lovers, we should be thankful there are both.

Right and far right Suntory Whisky chief blender Shinji Fukuyo accepts an accolade for Hibiki 21 Years Old, a whisky that has won consecutively at the World Whiskies Awards. Nikka chief blender Tadashi Sakuma accepts awards for Taketsuru Pure Malt 17 Years Old, which won the World's best blended malt and the best Japanese blended malt.

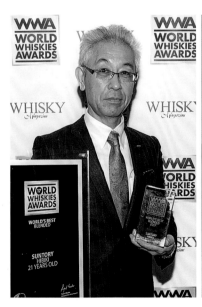

A Note about Spelling

Written in English, it's Japanese whisky, with no "e," reflecting its Scottish heritage where "whisky" typically is "e"-less on bottles and labels. In Canada, Ireland and the United States, the popular spelling is "whiskey," with an "e." But this distinction isn't always iron-clad. For example, Americans have used both "whisky" and "whiskey" spellings. The discrepancy is now a way of separating the different traditions. However, for Japanese whisky, the spelling isn't only a way to acknowledge Scotch's influence but is also part of the word's linguistic history in Japan.

In 1814, an early English–Japanese dictionary was published in Japan. Commissioned by the Dutch, who were at that time the only Westerners allowed to trade in Japan, the dictionary was somewhat useless for those hoping to communicate with native English speakers since words were written with Dutch pronunciations. Notably, it also did not feature the word "whisky," perhaps because the Dutch are traditionally gin drinkers. The first proper English–Japanese dictionary, however, did. Released nearly 50 years later, in 1862, it was compiled by Tatsunosuke Hori, a translator during Commodore Perry's visits. Between "whisker" and "whisper," there is an entry for "whisky," written with no "e." (At that time, whisky's spelling was still fluid in the UK and the US and the word was written with and without the "e" in both countries.) The 1862 dictionary defines whisky as "the name of a strong drink." Sounds about right.

In Japanese, the now standard way to write whisky is ウイスキー (uisukii). In the early 20th century, however, there were numerous ways to write whisky, such as ウイスキ (uisuki), ヰスキー (wisukii) and ウヰスケ (uwisuke). When Kotobukiya (now Suntory) launched the first true Japanese whisky, Shirofuda (White Label), "whisky" was ウ井スキー (uisukii), with the kanji character 井 (i) meaning "well" as in "water well." In the decades after World War II, Suntory changed to the standard ウイスキー (uisukii).

During its early years, Nikka also wrote ウ井スキー (uisukii), mixing kanji and katakana. Simply put, Japan's complex writing system uses kanji for ideographic writing, hiragana characters to conjugate verbs and in lieu of kanji, and katakana characters for imported foreign words, such as "whisky," and onomatopoeia. So when Nikka wrote whisky as ウ井スキー (uisukii), mixing the kanji character 井 (i) for "well" with phonetic katakana characters, it was reinforcing Masataka Taketsuru's belief that good whisky needed good water. Today, however, the official way Nikka writes whisky is ウヰスキー (uwisukii), using the obsolete Japanese katakana character ヰ (wi), which was originally based on the kanji 井. Why did

Three different spellings for "whisky" in Japanese: a poster for Nikka's first whisky released in 1940, a Torys billboard from the 1960s, and a present-day Nikka advertisement in Sapporo.

Nikka change? The official reason is that when the company registered its corporate name, Nikka Whisky, in 1952, it used the Japanese katakana character ヰ so that it didn't mix kanji and katakana characters in the same word, which isn't done in standard Japanese. The idiosyncratic ウヰスキー (uwisukii) appears on Nikka's website and the Yoichi Distillery gate. However, the earlier style ウ井スキー (uisukii) is still at a Yoichi photo op spot. Also note that the standardized uisukii (ウイスキー) is in small print on all Nikka bottles, as on all domestic whiskies for the clarification of consumers.

While these variations in Japanese might be the closest the country has to the English language whisky vs whiskey hullabaloo, this book follows the accepted regional spellings—"whisky" for Japanese, Scotch and Canadian, and "whiskey" for American and Irish.

Japan's Whisk(e)y History Begins

On July 8, 1853, four American warships sailed into Tokyo Bay with smoke billowing out of their coal-fired steam engines and with US guns aimed at the coast. The Japanese called them *kurofune* (黒船), or "black ships," and even today the term is used to describe something that comes from the outside and shakes things up. While this was not America's first contact with Japan, Commodore Matthew C. Perry wanted to force open the country to diplomatic relations and trade. In the 1630s, Japan kicked out the Portuguese missionaries and began an isolationist policy known as *sakoku* (鎖国), or "locked country," limiting international trade to the Dutch, Koreans and Chinese.

When warnings to turn back went unheeded, Japan didn't have much choice but to relent. In the days that followed, samurai boarded Commodore Perry's steam frigate to begin talks. The Americans, with their Manifest Destiny and gunboat diplomacy, were unwelcome guests, but aboard their ships they did what any proper host would do and served them refreshments, in this case American whiskey. From the sound of it, the distilled drink was a hit. According to the official US report, at least, the samurai bureaucrats "seemed to relish" the Western spirit, mixing it with sugar and guzzling "plentiful draughts."

Commodore Perry left Japan on July 17, 1853, but he returned the following February with more boats, more men and more booze. To show off Western superiority, Perry also brought presents for the Emperor and other top-level samurai. But Commodore Perry had no idea who the real Emperor was or what he did, thinking he was meeting with Imperial aids and not representatives of the Shogun, Japan's de facto ruler. Thanks to Dutch books, reports and maps, the Japanese knew a lot more about the Americans than the Americans knew about them! The actual Emperor, over 200 miles away in Kyoto, would not have wanted the gifted barrel of American whiskey (or the champagne, the telescope, the muskets, the Calvary swords, the pistols, the perfume, the books or anything else that the Yanks brought). All Emperor Komei wanted was for the Americans to leave, and he spent the rest of his life praying that those barbarians would do just that. He would've been aghast to learn that his son, the future Emperor Meiji, known to polish off several bottles of champagne in an evening, not only loved foreign booze but ruled during the country's push to modernize and Westernize.

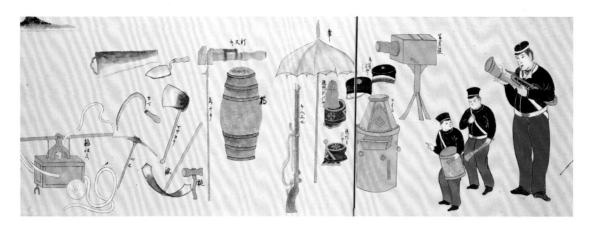

Opposite Samurai and naval officers sharing food and drink aboard the USS *Powhatan*.
Above A Japanese folding screen, hence the fold down the middle, estimated to date between 1853 and 1868, showing the gifts that Perry's expedition brought. In the middle is a cask, presumably one filled with American whiskey. (Historiographical Institute, University of Tokyo)

While Emperor Komei was not pleased, his loyal samurai were getting hammered. On March 27, 1854, only days before the two countries inked their first diplomatic treaty, the Americans held a shindig aboard the USS *Powhatan* for their Japanese counterparts. In his memoirs, crew member J. W. Spalding gave a vivid retelling of the lavish banquet, which started with a bang, literally. After a howitzer demonstration, dinner was served, but it was the drinks, Spalding noted, that made the Japanese delegates much more sociable. "With such a people, John Barleycorn is very potent: particularly in treaty making," Spalding wrote.

"John Barleycorn" is a personification of barley and the alcoholic drinks it makes, namely malt beer and whisky. Because the great Scottish poet and whisky aficionado Robert Burns had published a version of the ballad in 1782, this led to Japanese whisky writer Mamoru Tsuchiya claiming that both American whiskey and Scotch were served. Maybe, but in 19th-century America "John Barleycorn" did not exclusively refer to Scotch whisky. There are instances of it meaning beer and even US whiskey. For example, on August 30, 1854, the *Washington Telegraph* wrote, "The President of the United States,

amongst other presents to the Emperor of Japan, has sent him a barrel of American Whisky [sic]," adding that the paper wanted to know to what effect the "republican John Barleycorn" had on the Emperor. Here "republican" refers to America's democratic government in contrast to Japan's imperial ruler. There doesn't appear to be a surviving record of what kind of American whiskey this was. Since the Americans brought beer as well, this could also be the "very potent" John Barleycorn drink Spalding mentioned. Beer wasn't new to the Japanese because the Dutch had previously introduced it. However, one Japanese account from Perry's arrival compared the gifted brew to "horse piss."

Whatever was served, American whiskey, Scotch or "horse piss," the event sounded like quite the soiree. Commodore Perry later recalled that after the banquet, as the then thoroughly sauced Japanese delegates were leaving the ship, one of them threw his arms around the Commodore, saying, *Nichibei doushin* (日米同心), which was translated for Perry as "Nippon and America, all the same heart." In his drunken embrace, the samurai crushed the Commodore's new epaulettes.

Smoke billows from an American kurofune (black ship) in this 19th-century Hiroshige woodblock print.

The Local Drinks: Sake and Shochu

Before US whiskey ever arrived—or any of the other Western beverages that predate Japan's whisky debut, such as wine, beer and gin—Japan already had its own drinking tradition. Too often Japanese whisky is introduced in a liquid vacuum. To fully appreciate the drink, it's necessary to understand what are now considered the country's local spirits and brews and how they've directly and indirectly impacted Japanese whisky.

SAKE

The term "sake" is now widely used in English but in Japanese *sake* (酒) and the more polite *osake* (お酒) can also refer to all alcohol. For clarity, *nihonshu* (日本酒), literally "Japanese alcohol," is used to avoid any confusion when talking about sake, the drink, and not all alcohol. Third-century Chinese accounts mention that the Japanese loved the liquid, while the country's oldest written chronicles dating from the 8th century mention sake. It's used in religious ceremonies and celebrations and represents the soul of Japanese culture.

Even though whisky couldn't be more different, as late as the 1950s English language writers continually defined sake as "Japanese whisky." There is a historical precedent. Ranald MacDonald, a Scots American adventurer, risked death to barge into Japan through an unauthorized port in 1848, earning enough local trust to teach English to samurai, which would be tremendously helpful when the American Navy arrived the following decade. MacDonald later described sake as being "very like whiskey," incorrectly explaining that it was "a distillation from rice." The official report of Commodore Perry's expedition also made the same mistake, calling sake "a sort of whisky distilled from rice." It's likely they assumed that sake was distilled because most whisky is clear.

Made from rice, sake is brewed. Grains of rice are finely polished, steeped in water and steamed. With the help of a

Top Brewers at Kiyotsuru Shuzo in Osaka wash rice with a 35 percent polishing ratio for premium sake.
Above Steamed rice is cooled for *koji-kin* inoculation.
Left Rice is steamed in a tub called a koshiki, which was traditionally made of Japanese cedar.

fungus known as *koji-kin* and a yeast starter, the enzymes are broken down, turning starches into sugars. Sake's fermentation process, a necessary step in alcohol production, is far more complex than whisky or beer's. However, in Japan it's not uncommon for distillers to have a background in sake, often coming from brewing families or working as master brewers. The first Japanese to work in the American whiskey business, Jokichi Takamine, came from a sake-brewing family (for more, see page 24), while Nikka founder Masataka Taketsuru, who's hailed as one of the fathers of Japanese whisky, also came from a sake-brewing family. The sake connection continues today. Ichiro Akuto, the man behind the Chichibu Distillery, comes from a long line of sake brewers, while the master distiller at the White Oak Distillery in Akashi made sake for decades before also distilling whisky. Sake is different, yes, but sometimes its influences do find their way into Japanese whisky distilleries. Many Japanese whiskies, however, typically have an elegant and pleasant mouth feel that is reminiscent of that found in sake or even wine.

SHOCHU

Compared with sake, whisky has more in common with *shochu* (焼酎), with the word itself literally meaning "burnt alcohol." The drink and distillation might have come to Japan from China where, depending on who you ask, distillation was invented. (Another theory is that it came through Southeast Asia via Okinawa, then an entirely different kingdom, and into Japan's main island.) The first surviving direct mention of shochu is from the 16th century and was found in a Shinto shrine in Kagoshima, a region now famous for the liquor. Two carpenters wrote on a wooden plank that the shrine's head priest was so cheap that he never gave them any shochu. Traditionally, shochu was made at home, much like early Scotch. The shochu industry didn't emerge until the late 19th century when companies started distilling and selling the beverage. Today, many of the best shochu distilleries are in Kyushu Prefecture and produce excellent stuff. For much of its history, shochu was unfairly seen as a drink for drunks or the lower classes but was embraced by polite society during the white liquor boom of the 1980s. By 2003 it started outselling sake for the first time.

Honkaku shochu, or genuine shochu, can be made from a wide array of possible main ingredients, such as rice, barley, sugarcane, buckwheat, sweet potatoes, carrots, kale, tomatoes, chestnuts and even cactus. After the main ingredient is steamed, it's then added to a fermented mash inoculated with koji-kin, a micro organism native to Japan that turns rice starches into sugar (think malted rice), and then fermented once again before typically being distilled once, while *korui shochu* is made via a continuous still and has less flavor and character. Honkaku shochu is typically distilled in a steel pot still, but there are also copper pot stills for shochu that look like whisky stills—some of them even were! This is one reason why barley shochu, or *mugijochu*, is perhaps the most similar to whisky. (In recent years, peated mugijochu has even started to appear in stores. For more on peat, see page 34.) Walking around a mugijochu distillery might evoke the sights, sounds and smells of a whisky distillery, including a cask-filled shochu maturation warehouse with the soft, sweet scents that are so familiar to whisky aficionados.

Maturation, however, is typically shorter than for whisky, and the sweet spot for shochu is usually anywhere between a month to three years. There are exceptions, of course, but generally the spirit isn't aged much longer than that, as

Clockwise from right Behind the earthenware pots, called *kame*, are wood stills. Workers peel spuds to make *imojochu*, a sweet potato shochu. Cooper Hirotsugu Hayasaka refurbishes a cask at shochu maker Satsuma Shuzo. This steel pot still at Wakashio Shuzo isn't made from copper like whisky pot stills.

distillers don't see much point because shochu drinkers, unlike whisky drinkers, do not expect to get a dark amber or even brown-colored beverage. Traditionally, shochu is matured in clay pots but aging the drink in wood is not new. During the mid-1950s, Den-en Shuzo was one of the first to age its barley spirit in oak casks for an extended period of time, while around that same time liquor maker Komasa Jyozo was maturing its double-distilled rice shochu, known as Mellowed Kozuru, in casks, bottling it at 41 percent, around double the usual strength. In the decades that followed, with whisky flying off the shelves, barley shochu makers were increasingly using wood maturation, making their drink more whisky-like. It didn't hurt that the Japanese government began giving shochu distilleries earmarks to make their own casks, breathing new life into Japanese coopering. Independent Japanese cooperage Ariake Barrel started out in 1963 making crates for sake bottles before moving on to shochu casks the following decade. It now supplies many smaller Japanese whisky makers, such as Mars Hombo and Eigashima Shuzo, who don't have an integrated production line like at Suntory or the Chichibu Distillery. Coopers who have worked in the whisky

industry are also able to find work making shochu casks and vice versa.

The oak casks used in the shochu industry are the same as those in the whisky industry, although shochu cask size is not standardized in Japan and can vary from distillery to distillery. Since shochu doesn't leave a strong smell, ex-shochu casks can be repurposed as Japanese whisky casks. Coopers who made casks for shochu can easily switch to making whisky casks and vice versa. Hirotsugu Hayasaka, for example, worked for over 14 years at Nikka as a cooper before making casks for shochu maker Satsuma Shuzo for nearly 20 more. His apprentice, Kenta Nagae, now makes casks at Venture Whisky's Chichibu Distillery. There is no question that the shochu industry has been influenced by the whisky business, but if Japan didn't have shochu makers things like procuring high-quality casks might be difficult for many small and medium-sized whisky distilleries.

"Shochu and whisky are the same," says Hayasaka. Well, they might not be *the* same but they certainly are kindred spirits, and among some in Japan's shochu business there is a feeling that shochu is in a category of its own under the larger whisky umbrella. Today, many shochu makers wish they didn't have to water down darker cask strength spirit to the 20–25 percent alcohol by volume for bottling. Some shochu producers even say they'd love to release their products at a higher alcohol by volume and even in darker hues than the light yellow or even clear colors traditionally associated with shochu. Basically, they'd prefer to bottle at cask strength. Long-time shochu drinkers wouldn't necessarily be alienated because the stronger shochu would be part of a new expanded range and not replace traditional shochu. However, shochu distillers might experience pushback from a Japanese whisky industry unhappy to see new local competition, hence the reluctance.

Above The maturation warehouse at Wakashio Shuzo has familiar whisky-aging cellar scents.
Left A cask is charged at Satsuma Shuzo, releasing flavor and aromas in the wood.

Foreign Drinks Invade Japan

Whether it was the Portuguese, the Dutch or the Americans, one thing they had in common was that when they arrived on Japanese shores they brought booze. Over time, this foreign sauce became part of Japan's own drinking culture. The country didn't just enjoy sipping these libations but over time set out to master making them.

YOSHU

Yoshu (洋酒) literally means "Western alcohol" but it refers to distilled spirits like whisky, brandy, gin, vodka and rum. Even if their origins are foreign, wine and beer are sometimes not classified as yoshu but instead have their own categories. Ever since the Portuguese stepped foot in Japan in the mid-16th century, bringing casks of fortified wine, there have been Western-style alcoholic beverages in the country. They were not, however, imbibed by the masses. But since these drinks have been in Japan so long, this might explain why they are not always grouped with yoshu.

The first Western spirit distilled in Japan was not whisky but gin. And if you are going to make gin, what the heck, why not distill brandy as well? In 1812, that's exactly what Hendrik Doeff, the Dutch Commissioner in Nagasaki, did. The Napoleonic Wars had cut off trade and Doeff hankered for a bottle of jenever, aka "Dutch gin." Using a simple still, he and a local Japanese magistrate tried to distill both gin and brandy and also attempted to brew beer. The results were mixed at best, and Doeff had to sit tight until the ships arrived. Interestingly, due to recent whisky shortages brought on by massive sales, Japanese makers like Nikka have turned to gin to help flesh out their spirits line-up. This makes sense considering the long history Japan has with the drink.

The term "yoshu" didn't appear until later, during the Meiji Period (1868–1912), when the *kanji* character *yo* (洋) was slapped on everything foreign and was thus exotic to the Japanese. During that time, the West became equated with things new and modern. There was *yofuku* (洋服) or "Western clothing," *yoraku* (洋楽) or "Western music," *yoshoku* (洋食) or "Western food" and *yogaku* (洋楽) or

Young fashionable women enjoy drinks at a "yoshu cafe," a bar serving foreign liquor and mixed drinks. This *Mainichi* newspaper photo dates from 1934. On the counter, the word "fruits" (フルーツ) is written right to left as was the style prior to World War II. Today, it would be written left to right.

"Western learning," the last of which increasingly replaced the older word *rangaku* (ラン学), which also meant Western learning but directly referred to the Dutch ("ran" is from *Horanda*, the Japanese way of saying "Holland"). The Japanese government first officially adopted the term yoshu in 1870. Today, yo (洋) continues to be widely used, and generally speaking the Japanese don't think too deeply about wearing yofuku, eating yoshoku or rifling through the yoshu section at their local supermarket.

As the century progressed, more and more whisky arrived in Japan although it remained largely for expatriate consumption. By the early 1860s, the first Western-style bar opened in Yokohama, advertising that it served bourbon, Irish whiskey and Scotch whisky. Around the same time, according to a German traveler named Margaretha Weppner, that port city was filled with foreign seamen drunk on whisky "in the lowest state of depravity and degradation," which sounds about right.

Much of Western life, however, was still a mystery to the Japanese. Yukichi Fukuzawa, a writer and translator who was so instrumental in the creation of modern Japan that his portrait appears on the 10,000 yen note, the country's biggest bill, was one of the first Japanese emissaries to visit the US in 1860. Regular Japanese still weren't permitted to travel abroad. Fukuzawa penned a guidebook called *Seiyo-Ishokujyu* (Western Ways of Living: Food, Clothing and Housing). Besides explaining all sorts of things Japanese readers would have found curious, like doormats and chamber pots, he also discussed food and drink, including whisky, adding that it was "too strong" to have with one's meal. There is a relatively recent claim that Emperor Meiji received a bottle of Old Parr blended Scotch whisky brought back from another diplomatic envoy to the US and Europe called the Iwakura Mission (1871–73). One version of this story has it that Tomomi Iwakura visited the Cragganmore Distillery, which makes the main whisky in Old Parr. However, spokespeople for the Japanese and UK branches of Diageo, which own the brand, don't know where this story originated and added that the company has no historical records to substantiate these claims. Old Parr wasn't even trademarked until 1909 in the UK and in 1921 in Japan. Cragganmore dates from around 1870 and it didn't make whiskies for Old Parr until 1989.

For much of the 19th century, brandy was the most popular liquor in London. That started to change after a phylloxera plague ravaged French vineyards in the late 1800s, crippling European wine production and making it impossible to distill brandy. In Parisian cafes, people were switching to a new national drink of choice, absinthe, while in London brandy drinkers were now into whisky and soda. The whisky business was booming in Scotland and Ireland, with new distilleries popping up like mushrooms. Mean-

Japan isn't only an excellent place to drink Japanese whisky but also Scotch. Besides exclusive releases like Royal Household, there are also numerous bars with excellent Scotch selections. Try Bar Augusta Tarlogie in Osaka's Umeda or Helmsdale in Tokyo's Minami-Aoyama.

while, Japan's nascent wine production was nearly wiped out in the mid-1880s after imported rootstock introduced the dreaded phylloxera pests.

What whisky brands were found in late 19th-century Japan? A variety, actually. According to records from 1871, Yokohama-based trading company J. Curnow & Co. was importing a "cat mark" (猫印 or *neko jirushi*) Irish whisky, among others. It's believed that this nickname referred to Burke's Irish Whiskey, which registered its cat logo in 1876 but had been using it since 1870. Those same records, unearthed by *Whisky Magazine Japan*, also list a "deer brand" (鹿印 or *shika jirushi*) whisky, which might have referred to Dalmore as the distillery had been using its now famous royal stag emblem since 1867. During the 19th century, J. Curnow & Co. was also the official agent for Andrew Usher's Glenlivet Whisky, the Crown Distillery out of San Francisco, and Robert Brown's Four Crown Whisky. Other trading companies in Japan imported brands like Catto's Blended Scotch Whisky, Braunschweiger Rye and E. A Fargo's Spirit of 76 Bourbon. These imports were not aimed at locals but at the country's expatriate community. At that time, whisky was still a foreign drink. This, however, would change.

The Japanese drink business evolved rapidly during the late 1800s, with companies starting to distill alcohol with new-fangled column stills. Denbe Kamiya, who set up his own liquor shop in 1880, imported one from Germany, using it to produce shochu, which is traditionally distilled once in a simple still. This "new style" shochu was reportedly served at his Tokyo nightspot, Kamiya Bar, in 1899, which specialized in foreign drinks and remains in business well over a hundred years later. His contribution to column still distillation in Japan laid the groundwork for Japan to distill Western spirits, even if real whisky making was nowhere to be seen. At that time, the whisky market in Japan was still tiny, so the notion of distilling a drink from grain and then aging it for several years seemed like a bad business move, especially when there were other ways to make phony whisky. Potatoes, for example, were distilled via column stills, and the resulting alcohol was then mixed with additives. *Kajitsushu* (fruit wine) was also distilled and matured to make fake whisky. Another way to make imitation tipple included mixing small amounts of imported Scotch with distilled alcohol and other additives. Now, it's easy to look down on this stuff but at that time in Japan this was cutting-edge beverage production akin to the 19th-century version of modern artificial flavorings.

Scotch makers weren't content to let these spurious articles slide, even halfway across the world. In 1907, a court case was brought against an Osaka yoshu dealer named Teigi Nishikawa for violating the trademark of James Buchanan & Co.'s "Black and White" blended whisky with forged labels and fake whisky. The case made international news, with the *Guardian* and *Reuters* covering the suit. James Buchanan & Co. had an authorized dealer in Yokohama and a registered Japanese trademark, and the country's courts eventually ruled in the Scotch maker's favor. But for most Japanese customers, faux whisky was good enough because most hadn't had the real deal. For the country's elites, it was not. That same year, in 1907, the Japanese royal family issued an Imperial warrant for Buchanan's Royal Household blended Scotch whisky, which had been especially made for the British royal family. Japanese royal family members weren't the only bluebloods to put in an order that year, as the Crown Prince of Greece did, too. In the archives of Diageo, which owns the Buchanan's brand, there are no records of how the Emperor Meiji first came into contact with the Royal Household blended Scotch, but as Christine McCafferty, Archive Manager at Diageo points out, it's possible that either he or one of his royal retainers came across the whisky at an international get together as the UK and Japan did sign international alliances in the early 20th century. Or perhaps the Emperor Meiji, a long-time fan of Western liquor, had the Imperial warrant issued simply because of the British royal family. Whatever the reason, this is proof Japanese elites had a taste for the amber liquid. Today,

Japan is the only place in the world where Buchanan's Royal Household is on sale to the general public.

Yoshu expansion found an unlikely ally among makers of Japan's national drink, sake. As the century drew to a close and Japan continued to modernize, many sake breweries began consolidating, forming larger conglomerates. Sake production is traditionally during the fall and winter months, so these large companies began investigating ways to expand their portfolio and offer product that was not seasonal.

Besides being trendy and cosmopolitan, Western alcoholic beverages fitted that bill. Imitation whisky arose out of that need, with outfits like Osaka's Settsu Shuzo (*shuzo* (酒造) literally means "alcohol maker" but can refer to a brewery or distillery) producing fake yoshu. According to former Settsu Shuzo president, Kihei Abe IV, now in his mid-nineties, the company made something called "Alp Whisky"—that's right, no "s" in Alp. Abe says the drink was in the Scotch style but he isn't sure exactly how it was made when his grandfather, Kihei Abe II, was in charge. That might be for the best. However, as Japan inked more alliances with the UK and as more real whisky entered the country, drink makers knew that customers would eventually become savvier and reject their fake drinks. One young chemist in charge of making phony yoshu at Settsu Shuzo would help change Japanese whisky forever. His name was Masataka Taketsuru, and Kihei Abe II sent him to Scotland to study whiskey making.

An empty Settsu Shuzo yoshu bottle sits atop an advertisement for the company's *mirin* (rice wine for cooking). It's likely the bottle contained imitation whisky.

The Scottish Connection

"If you compared Japanese whisky to bourbon and Scotch whiskey, then obviously it is closer to Scotch whiskey," says Suntory chief blender Shinji Fukuyo. The general process—the malting, saccharification, fermentation, distillation and maturation—are similar to the methods developed in Scotland. There are, of course, Japanese twists on the process that help give Japanese whisky its own character. Even though Perry's expedition gave Japanese elites an early taste of the American stuff, why is the connection to Scotland so strong?

Perhaps because some of the most influential foreigners in Japanese history were Scots, most notably Thomas Blake Glover, aka the "Scottish Samurai." Arriving in 1859, a then 21-year-old Glover was an agent for the Hong Kong trading company Jardine, Matheson, and Co., sent to Japan to purchase green tea but who ended up running guns for samurai rebels. (Incidentally, the firm's co-founder, Alexander Matheson, used money he made from selling cotton, tea and opium to found the Dalmore Distillery in the Scottish Highlands in 1839.) Among his numerous accomplishments, Glover oversaw the construction of the country's first modern coal mine, invested in what became Kirin Brewery and was instrumental in the early days of Mitsubishi.

Or perhaps it was because in the late 19th century Scottish engineering and scientific innovation were world-class. Japan established close ties with Scottish academia during the Iwakura Mission (1871–73), with elites in the ensuing years going to Glasgow to study. While in Scotland, some students no doubt developed a taste for Scotch whisky! When Masataka Taketsuru went to Scotland,

there was an established tradition of his country's best and brightest going to the United Kingdom. While his visa might have said that he was in Scotland as a chemistry student, he was there for another purpose—to study Western booze.

Taketsuru grew up in Hiroshima in an upper-class sake-brewing family. He and his siblings went to the best schools, but Taketsuru didn't graduate from what is now Osaka University. Instead, in 1916 he got a job at Settsu Shuzo, then one of the country's most famous mass-market alcoholic beverage makers, to learn the drinks business. Settsu Shuzo was already distilling but it wasn't yet making real whisky. Rather, it was making concoctions to replicate its aroma, or at least what the Japanese at that time thought whisky should smell like. With World War I over, the country's economy was booming and the middle class was growing. Just as the Japanese had become comfortable with Western clothing, it was thought that if they developed a taste for proper Western alcoholic drinks, perhaps they would shun imitators, thus killing Settsu Shuzo's business.

It wasn't only because of Taketsuru's sake background or his ability as a chemist to whip up faux swill that led to Settsu Shuzo selecting him. It was also undoubtedly his fluency in

Far left Taketsuru's well-worn personal copy of his whisky-making bible. Inside, the margins are filled with his notes and annotations.
Left The connection between Nikka and Scotland remains strong.

Far left Thomas Blake Glover not only helped establish ties between Japan and Scotland but was instrumental in Japan's industrialization. He died in Tokyo in 1911 and is now buried in Nagasaki, the city he called home.
Left Masataka Taketsuru and Jessie Roberta ("Rita") Cowan married in 1920. Rita became a naturalized Japanese. Her 1925 passport listed her previous nationality as British.

English. In a time when many Japanese had never seen a foreigner, Taketsuru grew up studying English, then a rare skill for his fellow countrymen and one that would help him as a young man trying to learn how the Scots made their whisky. In many ways, the cosmopolitan Taketsuru was a forerunner of the *mobo*, 1920s Japanese slang for "modern boy." Without his worldly interest and language ability, Taketsuru would've had an even tougher time during his travels that kicked off in July 1918 when he boarded a ship in nearby Kobe leaving for California, where he'd check out American wine making before making his way to Glasgow, Scotland. When he left Japan, Taketsuru later recalled in his autobiography that his parents were there to see him off as well as Kihei Abe II, President of Settsu Shuzo, and Shinjiro Torii, who founded the company that's now called Suntory.

Upon arriving in Elgin, Scotland, Taketsuru sought out J. A. Nettleton to teach him whisky making. Nettleton had written *The Manufacture of Whisky and Plain Spirit*, a book Taketsuru lugged around as his whisky-making bible. The expert offered a detailed crash course but there was one hitch—the fee. Nettleton wanted far more money than Taketsuru, whose company was footing the bill, could pay.

The enterprising Taketsuru soon found another apprenticeship at Longmorn, apparently free of charge. The distillery's general manager, J. R. Grant, welcomed the eager visitor, and on the first day Taketsuru showed up in a pristine white lab coat, which was hardly standard wear at that time. The young chemist probably made a curious sight but the Longmorn distillery workers patiently answered all his questions. In his notebooks, he made detailed schematics of pot stills and other equipment. He spent five jam-packed

Above After decades of extensive renovations, the original Yamazaki Distillery building looks very different from the modern structure that stands today. This circa 1937 photo shows the distillery's kiln.
Right Osaka native Shinjiro Torii was a brilliant businessman with a nose for blending.

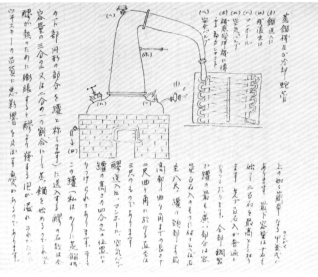

days at Longmorn where he learned how different casks could be used for different maturation periods, how caramel coloring was added to give a consistent hue to whisky and how spent mash could be sold for animal feed. Anyone else might have seen this as whisky-making minutia. For Taketsuru, it was the education of a lifetime.

More Scottish distilleries welcomed Taketsuru, a credit to Scottish generosity. Later, he spent much longer at Bo'ness in the Lowlands region and at Hazelburn in Campbeltown. During these apprenticeships, it's highly unlikely that anyone thought they were teaching a future rival. That would've been inconceivable, especially to Scottish distillers who never would've thought their biggest competitor would emerge from Japan of all places. Even if they did foresee this, which is highly unlikely, the distillers knew that there are so many variables in whisky production that even if Taketsuru started distilling his own whisky the result would be different from what they made. One can use the same ingredients, the same equipment and the same cask type but if the whisky is made in two different places you're going to get two different whiskies.

Taketsuru returned to Osaka in the fall of 1920 with a new bride, Rita Cowan, whom he had met in Scotland (see pages 90–91). He was ready to make proper whisky but poor economical conditions had convinced Settsu Shuzo not to distill the real deal. Taketsuru was back in the lab, concocting bogus stuff until 1922 when he quit the company that had sent him to Scotland. The following year he got a job at another Osaka drinks outfit, Kotobukiya, which translates as "Happiness House." Today, that company is Suntory.

Above left Taketsuru not only wore a white lab coat during his apprenticeships in Scotland but also throughout his career in Japan. **Above** Taketsuru took detailed notes on how a pot still worked, labeling each part. The upper right depicts a worm tub, which comprises a coil in a cold water tank that slowly condenses vapor back into a liquid.

The Birthplace of Japanese Whisky

The founder of Kotobukiya, Shinjiro Torii, had become a very rich man from the sale of Akadama Port Wine, a fortified wine he blended and released in 1907 to suit Japanese tastes. He thought whisky was going to be the next big thing and dreamed of distilling it in Japan. To do so, he hired the best people he could find, including Masataka Taketsuru, to set up and manage the country's first proper distillery. Taketsuru suggested several locations, such as Hokkaido Prefecture, located on Japan's northernmost island, because its climate was similar to Scotland's. Torii passed on this due to the high costs of transporting the whisky to the main island where lucrative markets like Tokyo and Osaka were located.

Other closer spots were considered, such as Yahata in Kyoto Prefecture, which Taketsuru wrote in his note-books would be "no good," Hirakata in Osaka Prefecture, which would be "okay," and Yamazaki, also in Osaka Prefecture, which Taketsuru wrote was "an ideal spot." All of his survey drawings included detailed notes of the nearest train lines and waterways. For Kotobukiya, it was important to find a spot that could not only produce quality whisky but one from where the whisky could be easily transported and sold, as well as a distillery that could be seen from the passing trains. Shinjiro Torii did not become a successful businessman by accident.

The result was the Yamazaki Distillery, Japan's oldest distillery, and Shirofuda (literally "white label"), the country's first real whisky, which would be called a single malt today. Cosmopolitan Tokyo might have seemed like a more logical place for Japanese whisky's birthplace, but as writer Masaharu Minabe explains in *The Birth of Japanese Whisky*, Osaka was inevitable. The city had a booming economy during the early 20th century, with prices that were lower than in Tokyo. More importantly, there were academic institutions in Osaka doing advanced research in chemistry and a number of the country's pharmaceutical companies were founded in the city. Combine that with

the city's rails and waterways, its central location within the country and its vibrant food culture, with savory soul food as well as traditional culinary influences, and it's no surprise that Japanese whisky was born in Osaka.

Taketsuru, however, would not stay in Osaka. After the failure of Shirofuda, he found himself running a Kotobukiya beer brewery outside Yokohama. But he hadn't traveled all the way to Scotland to learn how beer was made, and after his ten-year Kotobukiya contract was up, he struck out on his own, establishing his own company, Dai Nippon Kaju (Great Japan Fruit Juice), later shortened to Nikka.

Above Taketsuru took detailed survey drawings around Osaka and Kyoto for possible distillery locations. This sketch depicts Nishiyodogawa in Osaka, complete with rivers and the Hanshin train line. Taketsuru wrote 不適当 (*futekitou*) or "inadequate."

Above right Spotted at an Osaka bar, a collage of Taketsuru and Torii next to a modern version of the first whisky Nikka released in 1940, known as "Nikka Kakubin" or "Nikka Square Bottle." Suntory's Kakubin came out three years earlier.

Right Yamazaki Distillery workers pose with the first Japanese whisky in 1929. The man in the middle with the moustache is distillery manager Masataka Taketsuru.

The Revolutionary Sake-inspired Malting Process

Japanese whisky developed from the Scotch style. However, it could've become more American in character. And American whiskey could've ended up more Japanese if only Jokichi Takamine's novel malting process had caught on in the late 19th century. Takamine wasn't a whisky maker by trade but a biochemist. He was born in Toyama in 1854, only a few months after Commodore Perry left Japan, to a physician father and a mother from a sake-brewing family. The Takamines were well off, and from a young age Jokichi studied English with a local Dutch family, picking up their accent, which he had for the rest of his life.

After doing post-graduate work in Scotland and after marrying an American in New Orleans, Takamine figured out how to use *koji-kin*, the fungus sake brewers use to convert rice starch into alcohol on wheat bran. With this process, Takamine could break down the barley enzymes in only 48 hours instead of the typical malting period, which can take up to eight days, saving valuable time and meaning that distilleries could make sugar needed for the yeast to produce alcohol more quickly. No wonder the Whiskey Trust, then one of the biggest booze monopolies in the US, brought Takamine on board, making him the first Japanese to work in the whiskey business.

Everything started optimistically. On February 20, 1891, *The Chicago Daily Tribune* reported that, thanks to Takamine's malting technique, whiskey was going to be cheaper. It was later said his method would save three cents off every proof gallon. The process might've made whisky drinkers happy but it sure infuriated the maltsters, inciting protests. That October

a mysterious fire broke out at the distillery, torching all of the newly installed equipment. Takamine rebuilt and "Bonzai Whisky" apparently emerged from the ordeal. Professor Joan Bennett, a fungal geneticist at Rutgers University and a Takamine expert, saw the bottle in the 1980s at the archives of the now defunct Miles Laboratories, which had bought out Takamine's company. After Miles Laboratory was taken over by Germany's Bayer, however, the bottle of Bonzai Whisky appears to have gone AWOL. Donald Yates, then the archivist at Miles, recalls the curious "Bonzai" spelling and the bottle's yellow label. Was it supposed to read "Banzai" or "Bonsai"? What is clear is that the venture was a failure, Takamine's relationship with the Whiskey Trust went south and his koji-kin malting process never caught on. While his distilling days were a total bust, his other scientific research and business ventures were not. He isolated adrenalin, filed the first biotech patent in US history, earned millions of dollars and later funded the cherry blossom trees that now line Washington DC's Tidal Basin.

A postscript. When Masataka Taketsuru, the future founder of Nikka, was apprenticing at the Hazelburn Distillery in Scotland, distillery manager Peter Innes asked him about the koji-kin malting process. To test it, Taketsuru had the koji-kin, a powder that could easily fit in an envelope, shipped from Japan. According to Taketsuru Shuzo, his family sake brewery, it's unlikely he had it sent from home, but seeing how Taketsuru's then employer Settsu Shuzo also made sake, he probably had it mailed from their Osaka offices. In his autobiography, however, Taketsuru recalled that the experiment was not a success.

An older Takamine addresses factory workers. That's not whisky in the casks but polyzine, a diastatic extract used to degum textile mills. Takamine died in 1922. This image was taken in the late 1910s.

How Japanese Whisky Swept the World

Japanese whisky was no overnight success. There were false starts and failures, but relentless determination eventually resulted in greatness. Once scorned or looked down upon, and sometimes for good reason, Japanese whisky is finally getting the worldwide respect and adoration it deserves.

Early Attempts

Shirofuda was a disaster but Kotobukiya was keen to go international. In 1934, a year after Prohibition ended, it first began exporting whisky to the United States. Saying that Americans were not interested is being polite. A January 24, 1934 article in the *Chicago Tribune* about the first shipment of Japanese whisky coming to the US was anything but polite. "There are lots of horrible things I can conjure up in my lonely moments, but somehow Japanese whisky seems among the most terrible," the article went, adding, "Maybe it's Japanese Scotch! Could anything be more like a nightmare, more horrific in every sense of the word than Japanese Scotch?" There was no thought that Scottish distillers had been perfecting their craft for generations while Yamazaki was still finding its feet. Japanese whisky didn't have a chance in the US, and the prospect of World War II looming on the horizon certainly didn't help.

It did, however, in Japan. Whisky was ideal wartime sauce because it's high proof and keeps well. During World War II, both Kotobukiya and Nikka were mobilized, producing whisky for the Imperial Navy, with anchors on the label and all. But they didn't just make booze. Suntory set up a distillery in Okinawa to produce fuel alcohol for Japanese fighter planes, while in Hokkaido Nikka made a sweet wine in order to produce a crystalline form of tartaric acid, found naturally in grapes, for military radar production. This wasn't unusual as other large drink makers, such as Takara Shuzo, were also enlisted to make fuel alcohol for Zero fighters and whisky for Japanese servicemen.

Since both the Yamazaki and Yoichi distilleries were military factories, whisky production continued thanks to barley and coal rations. The town of Yoichi, a naval port, was bombed but the distillery was left unscathed. While Osaka City was firebombed, the Yamazaki Distillery's rural location and close proximity to Kyoto, which the Allies left alone, meant it made it through World War II intact. At the war's end, it was one of the area's few military factories that retained large raw material stockpiles as well as casks of whisky which had been squirreled away in a root cellar.

During the US Occupation (1945–52), Japanese whisky did reach an international audience again—albeit an audience that consisted of the American military. Kotobukiya, for example, began selling "Rare Old Whisky" which, according to its label, was "specially blended for American Forces," as well as "Blue Ribbon Whisky," a brand that seems to have beeen inspired by Pabst Blue Ribbon. Suntory Whisky, in particular, found favor among the officer class.

The whisky at Yamazaki was the real deal, but that wasn't true of every stockpile. According to an American press wire filed from Fukuoka in February 1946, the 32nd division US troops discovered a warehouse with Suntory bottles filled with what they thought was whisky. Oddly, the labels reportedly read in Japanese "Do not drink until reaching the sea coast" and the liquid inside appeared milky. After experiencing a rough hangover, the troops had a bottle analyzed. The drink was a "special tonic" for pilots on *kamikaze* missions, and lab analysis revealed it contained Benzedrine, strychnine and cocaine. Whisky, it wasn't.

Not all post-war whisky was fit for consumption. In December 1945, the head of the American military police in Tokyo warned of a Japanese whisky called "Red Heart" that was blamed for causing seven deaths in the metropolis, while there was also a report of Allied troops seizing 57 bottles of

The bottom of this Suntory Kakubin Whisky advert, which dates from 1950, states that there are also pocket-sized bottles available.

fake Scotch that had enough methanol to blind or kill. These dangerous, craven imitations appeared as daily goods became scarce and expensive as the war drew to a close. It wasn't affordable either. By September 1945, a bottle of Japanese whisky had gone from 2 to 3 yen to anywhere from 350 to 500 yen on the black market, while a bottle of imported Scotch had jumped from 7 yen to 1,000 yen. As the country began to rebuild, prices came back down to earth and Japan found itself with a whole generation of whisky consumers that continued long after the conflict ended.

Yet, even as Suntory started winning over Allied troops, like most Japanese products in the post-war era, the rest of the world still didn't take Japanese whisky seriously. As with Japanese cars, it would take decades for people's notions to change.

Japan Embraces Whisky

In the years after World War II, Japan's drinking scene boomed. According to Brewed in Japan, the country had 25,600 eating and drinking establishments in 1944. By 1959, there were over 186,000 more. The first Torys Bar opened in 1950 in Tokyo's Ikebukuro neighborhood, serving Suntory's budget-priced Torys whisky and peanut snacks. Aimed at average folks, Torys Bars were places people felt comfortable entering. In the decades that followed, over 2,000 Torys Bars opened across Japan but today only a few remain. Whisky consumption climbed yearly (it would increase over 500 percent by 1980), and while beer overtook sake, with home consumption increasing thanks to refrigerators becoming standard middle-class appliances, whisky was no longer seen as foreign, exotic or for the elite. It still had a regal image, but whisky was Japanese. Rivals like Takara Shuzo, Sanraku Ocean and Toyo Brewing all made whisky, with Toyo aging its stuff in a cave the Japanese Navy had used to store manned torpedoes!

Young Japanese men had began drinking whisky like never before during the war, acquiring a taste for it while in the military. Women were also drinking more *yoshu* in the post-war decades. According to the *Mainichi Shimbun*,

Left to right Prince Nobuhito, Emperor Hirohito's younger brother, visits the Yoichi Distillery in 1955, checking out newly made casks. The prince takes a tour of a Yoichi warehouse. With Masataka Taketsuru standing behind him, Prince Nobuhito looks into a microscope at the distillery lab.

the number of Japanese women drinking yoshu increased further by the late 1960s, thanks to affordable whisky served at trendy Tokyo bars. As the country's economic miracle kicked into high gear, the Japanese whisky business once again looked to go global, with Suntory leading the charge. Things seemed promising. Japanese whisky was getting reappraised, just as the country was reinventing its image, with the *Associated Press* writing in September 1958, "The best Japanese whisky deserves a better description than just 'imitation Scotch.'" In the US, Suntory Old's print ads from the 1960s now seem overblown, with lines such as "Like other classic arts of Japan, Suntory claims an ancient heritage. It is made by artisans whose ancestors distilled the world's first spirits more than 2,000 years ago." Suntory was reinventing Japanese whisky for a country that only a decade earlier had been an adversary, appealing to a romantic, pre-World War II image of Old Japan. Marketing spin aside, Suntory was also trying to make the best whisky it could.

During the 1970s and 1980s, bars called "snack," which served light eats, flourished in Japan as did hostess bars, staffed by young women in evening wear, ready to light cigarettes, flirt and pour whisky. At these bars, as well as at more "drinks only" type places, a pre-paid system called "bottle keep" became standard. Patrons would buy a bottle of their favorite whisky directly from the bar at a slight mark-up on the condition that whenever they returned they would have drams and drinks. The bottle system continues to this day and it not only at hostess clubs but also at more conventional establishments, like Hiro near the Yamazaki Distillery. "I think the bottle keep system wasn't only a status symbol, but a way to ensure what you were drinking and weren't getting duped by a questionable bar," says Hiro's Tatsuya Kitazawa. "Also, there is something special about sharing your own bottle with a co-worker or client."

Boom Goes Bust

In the decades after World War II, Japan had become the world's second largest economy. At home, the whisky business was booming. In 1976, Suntory alone churned out 255 million bottles of whisky (of which 85 million bottles were Suntory Old), but only 4–5 percent was exported. It was shipping its stuff to 68 different countries but focusing on the US, Central America and South America. Suntory began selling its whisky in the United Kingdom in the late 1960s, and by 1977 its whisky could be found at luxury London department store Harrods, though most ended up at Japanese restaurants. A decade later, a Suntory Royal Whisky billboard overlooked Times Square, but still only a small percentage was sold at export. Back home, the domestic business was so good that by the mid-1980s upstart distilleries began churning out *ji-uisukii* (地ウイスキー), or "local whisky," designed to give consumers a wider choice.

Scotch makers were keen to crack the Japanese market, which they decried as protectionist. In 1983, Japan's total whisky output peaked at 379,000 kiloliters (100,121,208 gallons), but then declined as white liquor like vodka and gin took off in a decade that equated "clear" with "healthy." The yen spiked in value after the 1985 Plaza Accord, causing a recession. By the early 1990s the Japanese economic miracle was over, ushering a "lost decade" of stagnant growth, and in 1996 the Scotch whisky industry won a World Trade Organization ruling that eliminated Japanese taxes on foreign whiskies which protected the local liquid. Previously pricey Scotch was cheaper than ever and Japanese whisky sales continued to flag. By the early 2000s now iconic distilleries like Hanyu and Karuizawa were casualties.

If Japanese whisky sales were bad at home at the turn of the century, the drink was still largely ignored abroad. But after a decade of drinking white sprits, such as vodka and gin, Scotch started getting yet another look-in during the mid-1990s, especially high-end single malts. By the late 1990s so was Japanese whisky. For example, Horst Luening, the master taster at online retailer Whisky.com, sampled Japanese whisky in 1999 when his company started selling the 12-year-old Yamazaki single malt. "The price was quite steep for 'only' a 12-year-old whisky. But after the first tasting we were convinced that the quality was high and the price justified."

Conquering The Whisky World

In 2001, Japanese whisky started to put numbers on the board when Nikka won its first international award. It also got an international push from Sofia Coppola's 2003 film *Lost in Translation*, in which Bill Murray played a washed-up movie star in Japan to film a Hibiki whisky commercial, in which he said "For relaxing times, make it Suntory time." This riffed on the long tradition of foreign celebs cashing in on Japanese commercials, especially whisky ones. Sofia's father, Francis Ford Coppola, had appeared with director Akira Kurosawa in a series of Suntory whisky ads in 1980.

After bottoming out in 2006, previously sluggish Japanese whisky sales started to rebound. The highball boom kicked off in 2008, thanks to a series of Suntory commercials starring super model and actress Koyuki of *The Last Samurai* fame. Once again it became fashionable among young Japanese women to drink whisky and soda. More international awards and praise followed. Everything seemed to reach fever pitch in Japan after *Massan*, a television drama about Nikka founder Masataka Taketsuru, began airing on television in 2014. This was followed the next year with famed reviewer Jim Murray hailing a Yamazaki Single Malt Sherry Cask as the best whisky in the world. Thanks to a slew of awards and new fans, Japanese whisky was on its way to conquer all. Elusive international success was finally Japan's.

Left Late in his career, Orson Welles reportedly lost an advertising deal with a French cognac maker after its owner apparently discovered that the filmmaker's Nikka G&G whisky commercial was still airing.

Below In the early 1980s, British rocker Rod Stewart did a series of commercials for Nikka Black 50, with his hit "Oh God, I Wish I Was Home Tonight" being the whisky's theme song.

The Karuizawa Distillery: A Japanese Legend

A great distillery was once here. As of fall 2016, reminders of Karuizawa Distillery still remained. The first pot still, dating from its 1955 founding, stood out front, even if the brick furnace below it had been stripped. Buildings were leveled, the chimney came down earlier that year, and a large paved driveway waits for what's likely to be a faceless commercial development. The Karuizawa Distillery should not have ended up like this but, alas, it has.

The distillery was located on what was originally a vineyard. Its parent company—Karuizawa changed hands multiple times throughout its history—had revved up its Ocean Whisky brand production at its Tokyo and Shiojiri locations before bringing Karuizawa online in 1956. At one time, in the late 1950s and early 1960s, Ocean Whisky was the second biggest maker in Japan, only to be later edged out by a rapidly ascending Nikka. Business was so good *The Guardian* reported in December 1961 that Ocean was even looking to export to the United Kingdom. A decade later, in 1976, the Karuizawa Distillery launched the first branded single malt in Japan, though at that time the phrase "straight malt" was used. "Karuizawa threw out the perception that Japanese whisky had to be neat and tidy," says David Croll, co-founder of Number One Drinks.

"It was big and gruff and in-your-face." The distillery was famous for making its whisky from Golden Promise barley and using sherry casks for maturation. The location, at the foot of an active volcano, is breathtaking. The average yearly temperature is 7 °C (45 °F), with cool summers and snowy winters. For centuries, Karuizawa has been a favorite place for the samurai elites to summer, escaping Tokyo's humidity. It also means this is a good place for slowly maturing whisky, or rather it was.

After the whisky business peaked in Japan in 1983, things went from bad to worse, then even worse. The Karuizawa Distillery was mothballed in 2000 by Mercian Corporation, which came under Kirin's control six years later. The distillery was finally shuttered in 2011. During that decade, as Japanese whisky sales continued to be in the dumps, Tokyo-based importer and distributor Number One Drinks began bringing Karuizawa whisky to a worldwide audience. Croll and his co-founder, Marcin Miller, the former publisher of *Whisky Magazine*, had a contact at Mercian and were able to bottle whisky from individual Karuizawa casks. Reportedly, Miller even suggested buying the distillery, which its owners probably would never have signed off on. Instead, the land was sold to developers and the equipment was rumored to have been repurposed. That which remained was sold at auction. Shizuoka-based whisky distributor Gaiaflow ponied up 5.05 million yen (US$45,000 at the time of writing) at auction for Karuizawa's old equipment to use at its maiden Shizuoka Distillery, established in 2016. "After several years of bottling a cask at a time, we decided to raise the stakes and made an offer for the remaining stock," says Croll. "We purchased several hundred casks." According to Croll, it's difficult to give the exact number of casks. They were stored at Venture Whisky's Chichibu Distillery but are now at another location in Japan. Croll says "not very many" are left. The demand and astronomical prices reflect that.

"Personally, I'm a great believer in the old adage that whisky is made for drinking, but the greater role played by collectors and investors over the past few years is testimony to the generally higher profile that whisky enjoys," says Croll. "Nobody is being forced into paying these high prices, although some of the auction results do leave me feeling a little queasy. Having said that, a little part of me somewhere takes pride in the fact that Number One played a role in shining a spotlight on this neglected distillery." Karuizawa whiskies are now some of the most expensive ever sold at auction. Bottles continue to float around online, easily going for several thousand dollars. That is, if you can find them, which might be the most bittersweet thing of all. But will new whisky ever flow out of Karuizawa? "I guess nothing is impossible," says Croll, "but personally I would prefer that nobody ever distills there again as it would certainly be an anti-climax." Karuizawa's whiskies are now part of liquid lore.

Above One of the few relics of the Karuizawa Distillery is the first pot still.
Far left Number One Drinks bottles Karuizawa's whisky with beautiful Japanese art on the labels.
Left A 10-year-old single malt from Karuizawa's Ocean Whisky days.

How Japanese Whisky is Made

Not all Japanese whisky makers think the same. There is no singular Japanese whisky-making process per se because there are variations among the distilleries and different approaches. However, the Japanese style is generally compared to Scotch, the whisky upon which it was originally based. While both use similar production processes and equipment, Japan throws in a few unique twists.

The Grains

As in Scotland, Japan makes malt whisky from malted barley, while grain whisky is made from corn, rye and wheat. A bit of malted barley is also added in grain whisky production to help convert starch into sugar. Traditionally, barley is malted by hand. It's soaked in water and spread out on a malting floor, then turned by shovel. This, basically, tricks the barley grains into thinking it's spring and they start to sprout, releasing enzymes that aid in turning starches into fermentable sugars. To stop the sprouts, the barley is dried by either hot air for unpeated whisky or with peat smoke for peated whisky. Those tiny particles glom onto the barley and then carry over those distinctive notes through distillation. These days, however, most barley is malted by industrial machines.

Barley is the grain that makes single malts happen. Pictured is imported malted barley, a staple of the Japanese whisky industry.

Japanese distilleries typically use imported malted barley, which can be ordered peated or unpeated (for more on peat, see page 35). The malt is milled and steeped in hot water, breaking down the grain's starches and creating a sugary liquid called "wort." Combined with yeast, the mixture ferments for around three days. The yeast gobbles up the sugars, producing an unhopped beer called "wash" that's between 5 and 10 percent alcohol. The default preference in Japan is to get the wort as clear as possible by filtering liquid wort from the mash's solid bits, resulting in a wash that is fragrant with fruity and floral aromas for which Japanese whisky is famous. Some Scottish distilleries also use a clear wort, but many prefer a cloudy one as it results in nuttier scents from compounds known as lactones. While the preference is for clear wort, if necessary Japanese distillers do produce cloudy wort to make whisky.

As in Scotland, the term "single malt" refers to a malted whisky that is made at a single distillery. The age statement on whiskies indicates the youngest whisky in the bottle. Unless the label reads "single cask," all whiskies are blends of malt spirit contained in different casks. Whiskies without age statements are still aged but often contain younger and older stuff. Blended whiskies refer to those made by blending whisky from different distilleries. In Japan, however, those distilleries are almost always owned by the same company, unlike in Scotland where whiskies have traditionally been traded between different makers. A "single grain whisky" does not refer to a whisky made from one grain but, rather, a grain whisky made at one distillery. A "single blended whisky" refers to a whisky comprised of malt and grain whiskies from a single distillery. In Japan, there are "pure malt" whiskies, which are blends of malt whiskies from different distilleries, and this being Japan those distilleries are owned by the same company. "Pure malt" was previously used for Scotch but was banned in 2009. No such stipulation exists in Japan, where the term is still widely used.

For grain whisky, corn is the key ingredient, although other grains, such as rye and wheat, are also used. Since corn cannot be malted, it must be broken down in a cooker, with the resulting liquid being run through towering steam-filled column stills, producing an alcohol vapor that is condensed into spirit. The result is a lighter spirit with a high alcohol percentage. Japan's biggest makers have fine grain distilleries and their grain whiskies are the backbone of many of the country's most famous blends.

Water

Japanese whisky makers love to talk up their water, giving it an almost mythical quality, just like their counterparts in Scotland and the United States. Yes, the water near the Yamazaki Distillery in Shimamoto, Osaka,

Instead of dumping the yeast directly, as at many distilleries, at Nikka's Yoichi a concentrated yeast starter called shubo is made and then piped into the washbacks.

is so delicious that it's considered among the country's best. In Yoichi, locals are quick to offer a glass from the tap to prove just how good their distillery's water is, while the Kirin Distillery's production water is from Mt Fuji's melted snow filtered through lava, so it's got to be good, right?

"Soft water is most common in Japan, and it best suits traditional Japanese food like rice and fish," says Tsuyoshi Sanno, who joined Suntory in 1971 and until 2016 participated in the Suntory Natural Water Forest program, which does ground water surveys for production use. According to Sanno, hard water, such as the kind found in France, goes best with Western food, especially meat and bread.

Japanese whisky is often highly aromatic and floral. Even those with high phenolic levels often seem as smoky as the peat monsters coming out of Scotland. The different yeasts used in Japan might have something to do with this, but Suntory chief blender Shinji Fukuyo thinks the reason could be Yamazaki's water. That delicate softness, Suntory believes, results in a whisky that pleases the Japanese palate. Water might help bring out flavors and aromas during fermentation but there is an argument that the influence of water is minimized after fermentation, double distillation and lengthy maturation. But, as Sanno points out, good soft water is used to cut the whisky and bring it down to bottling

strength, so its importance cannot be easily discounted. The biggest impact water makes, however, is after the whisky has been purchased when consumers add it (or ice) to suit their tastes.

Yeast

To make alcohol, you need yeast. It's necessary for fermentation and feeds on the sugary wort, producing alcohol and natural aromatic, fruity-smelling chemical compounds called "esters." For Scotch whisky, there have traditionally been two kinds of yeast—distiller's and brewer's. Less importance is placed on individual yeast types because most Scottish distilleries use the same strain of industrial, mass-produced distiller's yeast, aiming for a high alcohol yield.

Japanese distillers, however, use an array of different yeasts to bring out specific aromas. Nikka uses several different yeasts, and while not confirming exactly how many, the maker said that it has fewer than 10 different kinds specifically for whisky. Suntory, however, has around 150 different yeast varieties. Kirin also has hundreds of unique strains. Each distillery can select the optimal strains to create certain aromas that then carry through to the final whisky. In this regard, Japanese whisky makers are similar to America's bourbon distillers, who likewise emphasize the importance of unique yeast strains.

Japanese whisky makers like Nikka, Mars Whisky and Eigashima Shuzo also create pure, concentrated yeast starters called *shubo* (酒母), a technique from sake production (see page 81). Making shubo complicates the process but gives distillers more control during fermentation, ensuring a high-quality wash. This interest in yeast is no accident. "Japan's culture of fungus is closely related to the weather," says Mars Whisky Shinshu Distillery manager Koki Takehira. The country's humidity breeds fungus and the Japanese have learned to use it to their advantage. Japanese use fungus on a daily basis during cooking, whether in making *miso* soup or eating those stinky fermented beans called *natto*. It's only natural that Japanese whisky production would have a deep understanding of yeasts and how they influence flavor.

Distillation

For malt whisky, distillation is done twice in pot stills. Japanese distilleries use a range of techniques when distilling, from direct to indirect heating of the stills. The Yoichi Distillery is the only place in the world that still fires its pot stills the traditional way—with coal.

Nikka, Suntory, Hombo Mars and Kirin use Made-in-Japan stills from Miyake Industries, which previously manufactured them for the former Hanyu Distillery. Today, small-scale distilleries, such as Chichibu and Akkeshi, however, import stills directly from Scotland, explaining that such stills better suit their needs.

Both Suntory and Nikka both produce high-quality grain whisky with each of their column stills, which are towering structures that might not be pretty but are workhorses,

Left At the Sun Grain Chita Distillery, grain whisky is made with continuous column stills. **Below** Distillate bubbles up in a pot still at Mars Whisky's Tsunuki Distillery. The second distillation produces a clear spirit that gets its color during maturation.

churning out continuous flows of distillate. The Kirin Distillery is in a league of its own in Japan, having a total of three different methods on-site for grain whisky—multi-column stills to make a light spirit, column stills and a kettle to make a medium-style spirit, and a beer column and a doubler to make a heavy, bourbon-style spirit. The last two distillation set-ups are unique among Japanese distilleries.

Since grain whisky facilities are often enormous, as tall as buildings, and because they are costly to install, only large makers like Suntory, Nikka and Kirin are able to make grain whisky in-house. Smaller Japanese distilleries don't have the equipment, and when they need grain alcohol for their blends they say they're unable to buy it from these larger Japanese whisky makers. Instead, they must import grain whisky from Scotland for blending. Mars Whisky, however, has begun using some domestic grain spirit.

Maturation

It's said that 70 percent or more of whisky's flavors and aromas come from the cask. Maturation not only smoothens out the spirit but also changes it from clear to shades of amber and brown, infusing it with the scents of honey, vanilla, fruits and more. In whisky making, casks are king.

The spirit produced by distillation is clear. Those amber to brown hues are the result of maturation in wood. However, most Japanese whisky is colored with natural caramel food coloring. If it's not on the label, assume that the whisky maker is keeping coloring an available option. Caramel color is also allowed under Scotch whisky regulations and is widespread in the Scotch whisky industry where it's been used for over a hundred years. The reason makers give for adding the coloring is to ensure a consistent color profile for consumers, because some batches might have lighter hues and picky consumers may complain. Only a tiny amount is used, and while whisky makers say people cannot taste the caramel coloring, it's a hot topic of debate among aficionados. Turning one's nose up at caramel coloring means you'll miss out on some of the greatest whiskies of Japan—and Scotland.

Japan, however, does not have rules about maturation length in the way Scotland does. But Japanese distilleries typically follow the three-year maturation bare minimum rule out of respect for the Scotch-making tradition and because whisky younger than that might not be so good. It's during maturation that the spirit interacts with the cask, pulling out flavors and aromas that exist naturally

in the wood, changing and influencing the whisky. Each year, a percentage of the spirit is lost in evaporation during the maturation process in what's called the angel's share, which has been translated into Japanese as *tenshi no wakemae* (天使の分け前).

As with other whisky makers around the world, the most common casks used for aging are made from American white oak. The wood is famous not only for its sturdy reliability but also for infusing the spirit with caramel, honey and vanilla notes. Most American white oak casks are former bourbon barrels, thanks to an American law that stipulates bourbon casks must be brand new and cannot be reused, thus creating a vital second-hand market. Sherry casks are also used in whisky maturation in Japan, like in Scotland, to impart delicious dark fruit flavors. A small percentage of Japanese oak (*mizunara*) casks are also used (for more, see pages 36–38). As in Scotland and elsewhere, wine casks are sometimes employed for what's called "finishing," in which a matured spirit finishes its aging period in a wine cask, adding extra flavors.

The importance of casks is why Japan's biggest whisky makers, Suntory and Nikka, have their own cooperages to main strict control over production. The same goes for the Chichibu Distillery, a rarity for a small Japanese outfit. It's not unusual for distilleries anywhere in the world to have coopers on hand to repair and remake casks, but these Japanese distilleries are all able to make brand-new casks to their exact specifications, giving them a unique degree of integration. With the price of casks going up, thanks to an increased whisky demand, it's becoming harder for distillers to get good ex-bourbon and, especially ex-sherry casks. Suntory, which owns Jim Beam, and Kirin, which owns the Four Roses Distillery, have no problem obtaining high-quality bourbon barrels, the key to whisky production. Since sherry consumption has remained static but whisky demand has shot up, ex-sherry casks are in high demand. Suntory is able to secure a steady stream of former sherry casks direct from Spain, another way it can maintain control over its whisky production. Other whisky makers rely on independent Japanese cooper Ariake Barrel for their needs.

Numerous variables impact flavor during aging, such as the size of the casks, with smaller casks speeding up the process because of greater contact with wood, the type of warehouse the casks are stored in, and even the exact location within the warehouse in which they rest. Those in the upper echelons of the warehouse age faster because of the heat, while those in the lower mature more slowly. You can put two casks in different locations in the same warehouse and end up with two different whiskies!

The Climate

Besides the wood itself, the local climate can influence a whisky's character. During cold weather, the cask contracts and the spirit seeps into the wood. Cooler climates result

The blender's lab at the Chichibu Distillery is filled with whisky samples Ichiro Akuto uses to create his whiskies. Each sample is labeled in detail so that Akuto will know not only when it was distilled but from which cask the spirit came.

in slowly aged whisky. When the weather heats up, the cask expands, pushing the spirit out. Distilleries located in hotter climates therefore mature whisky more quickly.

Weather across Japan is hardly uniform. Nikka's Yoichi Distillery, for example, sits on Hokkaido's western coast in the country's northernmost island, where it experiences long, frigid winters and mild summers. This results in a mellow aging process. Located at the foot of Mt Fuji on Japan's main island, the Kirin Distillery has a mild annual temperature of about 13 °C (55 °F), which was one of the reasons the site was chosen. Even though Nikka and Kirin, for that matter, like to point out how their distilleries are located in climates that are similar to Scotland's, these distilleries are not, in fact, located in Scotland. By default, both will produce different whiskies.

In other parts of Japan maturation happens much more quickly, such as at Suntory's Yamazaki Distillery in Shimamoto, Osaka Prefecture, or its Ohmi Aging Center in nearby Shiga Prefecture. This is why Suntory prefers larger casks for these locations so that the whisky doesn't age too quickly. The area's subtropical weather is closer in character to Kentucky's than Scotland's (no wonder Shimamoto's sister city is Frankfort, Kentucky!). This is why the Yamazaki Distillery, with its long summers and short, cold winters, will naturally produce a different whisky than Yoichi, with its long, frigid winters and short, mild summers. Likewise, Eigashima Shuzo, which is located nearly an hour from

Kobe, also has blistering summers. The distillery only makes whisky in late spring through July, and the climate most certainly influences the whisky. Eigashima Shuzo's White Oak Distillery is often cited as the Japanese malt whisky distillery that's closest to the ocean, while Suntory's Chita Distillery literally sits on an enormous industrial pier in Nagoya Port. The White Oak Distillery is rather picturesque. The Sun Grain Chita Distillery, in contrast, is not.

Blending

After the whisky is matured, Japan's master blenders go to work. Some are so fastidious about what they eat that they have the same thing for lunch every day to ensure a consistent palette! Others eat whatever they like, just short of spicy foods, prior to blending.

Cooking is a good way to think about the process. Japanese blenders often use peated whiskies to bring out other flavors, while not dominating the blend's profile. It's a technique that is reminiscent of how Japanese cooking uses sugar or a sweet sake called *mirin*, not to simply sweeten but to bring out other savory *umami* flavors in the dish.

Suntory uses grain whisky in its Hibiki blends akin to *dashi*, a broth made from dried *katsuo* (skipjack tuna), or *kombu*, used throughout Japanese cooking to underpin soups. Soup broths vary throughout Japan, and Suntory's lighter house style resembles broth common in Osaka and Kyoto more closely than the darker and heavier soup of Tokyo.

About Japanese Barley and Peat

Japanese distilleries mainly depend on imported malted barley, both peated and unpeated, from Scotland and elsewhere. Suntory and Nikka produce millions of liters of whisky annually, so using high-priced domestic barley doesn't seem feasible for mass production, especially as there is some dispute over how much barley impacts the final whisky's flavor.

Around the globe, it has become the norm for whisky distilleries to depend on commercial malters. Only a handful of Scottish distilleries still malt and peat their own barley and then only use a small percentage in their whiskies. Distilleries like Springbank, which does everything in-house, are a rarity. "Even Scotland can't produce all the barley the whisky makers there need and they have to import from places like Germany," says Mars Whisky's Koki Takehira.

Drying the malted barley at a distillery is largely a thing of the past, even in Scotland. A kiln's iconic pagoda no longer puffs out smoke, but rather, has become a symbol that proclaims "Whisky is made here." By the 1970s the Yamazaki Distillery ceased malting and peating its whiskies on-site while Nikka's Miyagikyo Distillery continued until the mid-1980s. The Yoichi Distillery still has a functioning kiln, which reeks of peat dug up from a Hokkaido moor, but as of writing the kiln is only used for demonstration purposes. Smaller Japanese distilleries are increasingly expressing interest in domestic grain and local peat. It's remarkable that a young distillery like Chichibu has a functional kiln and has taken up the painstaking traditional process of malting by hand.

Japanese Barley

For many decades Japanese whisky was made from Japanese barley. Until the early 2000s the Japan Spirits and Liqueurs Makers Association agreed to use a certain percentage of domestic barley in whisky production, but as the whisky market was skidding towards rock bottom that agreement was changed in 2004 to allow the Brewers Association of Japan to meet that percentage. Nikka, for example, doesn't make beer but is owned by Asahi which, according to Nikka chief blender Tadashi Sakuma, took over that obligation. Traditionally, the amount of domestic barley the Brewers Association of Japan buys is a verbal promise because drawing up a formal contract would violate global trade regulations.

In the years before World War II and the decades that followed, the most common type of two-row barley found at Japanese distilleries was Golden Melon, which was first brought to Japan by former Civil War cavalry officer and US Agriculture Commissioner Horace Capron, who came to Japan in 1870 as an *oyatoi gaikokujin* (お雇い外国人), basically a hired foreign advisor, to develop Hokkaido. Besides introducing new livestock and working on Sapporo's urban planning, he imported seeds from America, including Golden Melon, feeling it would suit Hokkaido's soil. That it did, and Golden Melon led to the birth of the Japanese beer industry, with the Sapporo Brewery setting up shop in 1876. The flavorful Golden Melon flourished first in the Japanese beer industry and later in the country's whisky business. The Chichibu Distillery in Saitama has come into possession of Golden Melon seeds and is running tests to see if it's possible to use the variety in a future release. Says Chichibu Distillery founder Ichiro Akuto, "It's hard to say how it will influence the flavor, but I'm curious to find out and taste it."

As with most types of heritage barley, Golden Melon doesn't have the high alcohol yield that modern bioengineered barley does, but it must have pleased Japanese whisky distillers and beer brewers because Golden Melon was the go-to barley for decades. During the 1920s at the Yamazaki Distillery, sacks of Golden Melon were stacked so high they seemed to reach the warehouse ceiling. Even as late as the early 1970s, Suntory advertised that it used "choice" Golden Melon barley in its Old Suntory whisky. When Masataka Taketsuru first established Nikka in the 1930s, and for decades afterwards, Golden Melon was used in the Yoichi whiskies. That was then.

"At Nikka, we still have older whisky that was made from Japanese barley, and I think using Japanese barley to make new whisky would make for an interesting topic of conversation," says Nikka chief blender Tadashi Sakuma. "However,

Far left Harvesting peat at a bog in Ishikari, Hokkaido.
Left Barley is a traditional crop that's been grown in Japan since ancient times. *Mugicha* or barley tea is an excellent summer beverage.
Below This field of Japanese barley will be used in domestic beer production. In Japan, barley and wheat are not harvested in the fall, but typically from May to June. This harvest is called *bakushu* (麦秋), with the *kanji* characters for "wheat" or "barley" and "fall."

certainly gives the drink a stronger sense of place and also allows distilleries further control over their final product.

Japanese Peat

Peat can give whisky a phenolic and smoky vegetation flavor. In Japan, distilleries order their malted barley already peated, specifying the parts per million of peat phenols that they want. Some distilleries go one step further, mixing peated and unpeated barley to suit their exact needs.

In the 1970s, English language journalists incorrectly stated that Japan doesn't have peat, with the *Guardian* writing on November 12, 1977 that "without the Scottish peat, the Japanese would be lost." Local peat's prospects weren't helped by Suntory advertisements in American newspapers stating that its whiskies were made with Scottish imports. But as with barley, Japan does have its own peat, which can be found all over the country. Due to World War II fuel shortages, peat was dug up in Japan as an energy source. Today, the country's largest island, Hokkaido, is peat central, with 6 percent of the prefecture's flatland covered in it. Until recently, workers at Nikka's Yoichi Distillery still dug up local peat every year to use for demonstration purposes. There are also Japanese companies that specialize in peat, such as the Takahashi Peat Moss Co. in Hokkaido, but it's not used for whisky production.

In an effort to stand out and to make as much of a domestic product as possible, smaller distilleries are looking to local peat to dry local barley. The Chichibu Distillery in Saitama is sourcing local peat, which it compares to the kind of peat found in the Scottish Highlands, and the newly opened Akkeshi Distillery in Hokkaido is currently studying the unique elements in its own peat. This might result in nuanced variations, but even if the differences are only marginal, this is part of a larger trend to make Japanese whiskies as local as possible or eventually take steps towards an "All Japan" release.

I don't really think the barley would have that much impact on the flavor." Sakuma points out that at distilleries around the world, the barley variety is constantly changing. "To me, playing up a certain type of barley or a particular water doesn't exactly seem truthful," he adds. "I'm not saying they have zero influence, but I wonder if people can discern it."

Japanese barley can be up to four times more expensive than imports, which is a figure to scare off many producers. Besides, competition for the local grain already exists among beer brewers, *shochu* distilleries and tea companies as well as other food companies, such as noodle and bread makers. There are Japanese maltsters, such as the Kanbaku Company in barley-rich Tochigi Prefecture, and they're typically connected to large drinks companies. Suntory founded Kanbaku back in 1961 to malt barley for whisky and beer and now the company is part of the larger Suntory Group. While Suntory does use a percentage of domestic barley for beer, it does not for whisky. This is a shame because even if the variations in flavors are nuanced, slight or barely noticeable, these differences could influence the whisky's character. This could be why smaller distillers are showing increasing interest in the domestic crop. The rise of craft beers also means it's easier, but certainly not cheaper, to get Japanese malt. Even if the flavor variations are only marginal, using home-grown barley in a Japanese whisky

Precious Made-In-Japan Casks

As the demand for whisky goes up, casks become pricier and harder to get. This means it's more important than ever to take excellent care of older casks. While many Scottish distilleries rely on second-hand casks, the giants of Japanese whisky, Suntory and Nikka, also make their own new, or virgin, casks. This gives them complete control over their production. Even Venture Whisky's Chichibu Distillery, one of Japan's smallest, has an on-site cooperage producing high-quality new casks.

But only a limited number of these virgin casks are used in maturing Japanese whisky, and just as in Scotland ex-bourbon barrels fill up the majority of distillery warehouses across the country.

"There aren't many Western-style coopers in Japan," says Hirotsugu Hayasaka, a master cooper who previously worked at Nikka Seidaru, the whisky maker's dedicated cooperage company. Former cooperages have either shuttered or retooled, like Fukui Yodaru, now a corporate logistics company, or Showa Yodal, which specializes in wood flooring. (A spin-off company, however, Showa Yodal Konki, works on-site at the Kirin Distillery, taking care of the barrels.) Maru S Yodaru, which previously handled casks for the Hanyu Distillery, is no longer in operation after its master cooper, Mitsuo Saito, retired. His equipment is now being used in the Chichibu Distillery's cooperage.

There are more *wadaru* (Japanese-style cask) coopers than *yodaru* (Western cask) ones. Japan's own cask-making tradition didn't begin until after the 14th and 15th centuries when the carpenter's plane was introduced from China. Japanese-style casks are cylinder-shaped vessels that are bound by split bamboo cane and don't have the bulging mid-sections of Western casks, instead can fan out slightly at the top. This style of cask isn't used in whisky maturation but, rather, *shochu* and sake aging. Traditional Japanese *sake-daru* (sake barrels) are made from Japanese cedar, which helps them impart a clean, fresh and sharp scent on sake. Since there are no Japanese regulations about which woods can be used in maturation, Suntory even uses a percentage of Japanese cedar to age whisky in its budget-priced Torys blend.

For smaller Japanese distilleries unable to make or even mend their own casks, there's the country's last remaining independent cooper, Ariake Barrel, which fills the void left by other cooperages that have left the business. Founded in 1973, Ariake Barrel got its start making crates for sake bottles. Most of its business lies in shochu casks, but increasingly it's been making more and more for whisky.

Ariake's cooperage in Kyushu is a flurry of activity, with over a dozen coopers churning out between 4,000 and 5,000 new and refurbished casks per year of various types and sizes, including rare Japanese oak casks. American-made

Far left Cask planks called staves are held in place by large metal hoops.

Center left A new cask is toasted before charring.

Left An Ariake Barrel cooper puts the final touches to a finished cask.

Right A shovel full of sawdust is tossed onto an open flame, causing fire to shoot through the cask. The cooper then turns the cask on its side, rolling it down the cooperage where the fire is extinguished with water.

bourbon barrels, for example, are generally functional and not much to look at on the outside, but perhaps since Ariake Barrel also has a history of making wine casks, which are traditionally handsome on the outside, it makes good-looking new casks. In years past, around 90 percent of Ariake's handiwork was used to age shochu. These days that's changing with more casks used for maturing whisky.

At Ariake, the charring is done the old-fashioned way, with casks placed over a small fire and a shovel load of sawdust thrown in, causing the fire to shoot up to the ceiling and the cask to catch fire. The burning cask is rolled, flames shooting out in spectacular fashion down the warehouse, and another cooper hoses the fiery cask with water. At other cooperages in Japan, it's more common to char casks by machine. Ariake relies on the experience of its craftsmen.

Mizunara: Rare Japanese White Oak

The majority of whisky, Japanese whisky included, is mostly aged in American white oak, followed in second place by European oak. However, Japan has its own unique and rare wood called *mizunara* (ミズナラ) or Japanese oak, that's used to make whisky casks, but in significantly smaller numbers. Japanese people outside the world of whisky might call mizunara trees *donguri no ki* or "acorn trees." But Japanese oak is much more than simply acorn trees. It's made into some of the most expensive and desirable whisky casks on earth. No wonder Scotch makers like Bowmore and Chivas Regal have done their own mizunara releases.

Mizu means "water" and refers to the moisture that the oak contains, while the word *nara* (楢) is "oak." Mizunara

is also known as *oonara* (大楢) or "great oak," and is closely related to *konara* (コナラ or 小楢), which literally means "small nara." However, konara doesn't grow as large as mizunara (obviously), and thus isn't as widely used in casks. Mizunara can be found all over Japan, including temperate regions such as Osaka. However, the Japanese oak that grows in colder climates, such as Hokkaido, has a tighter grain and closer annual rings, both of which are ideal for cask making.

When the Yamazaki Distillery began distilling whisky in 1924, after construction began in 1923, it only used sherry casks made from European oak, which imparts more dark fruit and spice flavors. At that time, sherry casks were the whisky maturation norm in Scotland, and Shinjiro Torii's wine business connections no doubt proved helpful in acquiring good sherry casks. When they became hard to import during World War II, the Yamazaki Distillery turned to mizunara casks. It was not the first to do so.

In Hokkaido, Japanese wine makers were already using mizunara casks by the 1870s. Beer brewers did likewise. The Japanese at that time weren't trying to bring out special characteristics with mizunara in the way that today's whisky distillers can. Rather, they needed wood for casks and Japanese white oak seemed sufficient. But mizunara wasn't only used to make casks. People built tables, chairs, sleds, wagon wheels, houses, you name it, from mizunara.

When cut, mizunara has wonderful markings that are fittingly called *torafu* (虎斑) or "tiger stripes." These appealing characteristics are why during the late 19th and early 20th centuries, mizunara was exported to the United

Kingdom to make desks, tables, hand railings, wood paneling and even toilet brushes and coffins! Exported mizunara was also used to make casks. In 1926, for example, the English-language *National Cooper's Journal* wrote how Japanese oak was "considerably used for high-grade barrels, especially for beer" in Belgium prior to World War I. However, a 1959 report from the Brewing Industry Research Foundation in the United Kingdom stated, "Japanese oak has been tried for making casks but it is said to have proved to be too porous to hold beer for very long."

While the Yamazaki Distillery only turned to Japanese oak because importing sherry casks became difficult during World War II, one of the reasons why Masataka Taketsuru picked Hokkaido to set up Nikka's first distillery in 1934 was the availability of mizunara. This is also why he brought the talented beer cooper Yoshiro Komatsuzaki, an expert in chopping and splitting Japanese oak for casks, to Yoichi. Mizunara continued to dominate Nikka's warehouses until 1965 when it began testing American white oak to mature its whiskies. Five years later, it switched over to the American wood because it is less prone to leak, and today it barely uses any Japanese oak. Yet, throughout the whisky business, no wood is more desirable and more expensive than mizunara. So what gives?

Why Mizunara is Special and … Difficult

Mizunara is not simply oak that grows in Japan. It expands the range of flavors and aromas in whisky. According to joint research between Suntory and Heriot-Watt University in Edinburgh, 27-year-old whisky aged in mizunara casks has a slightly different flavor profile from whisky aged in American oak. Japanese oak-aged whisky has fewer cereal, grassy and fresh fruit notes but is slightly feintier and has slightly more sulfury aromas that are described as a "struck match." This perhaps explains why whisky aged in mizunara is compared to the scents found in a temple or shine, such as incense or burning candles.

This Hokkaido University Library photo dating from September 1876 shows a Sapporo winery with mizunara casks stacked out front. Some of the men wear traditional garb though most are in suits.

Chemical analysis revealed that whisky aged in mizunara casks has a much higher rate of "coconut"-type aromas due to, it seems, a high concentrations of translactone than is found in whisky aged in American white oak. The research also shows that both coconut and incense aromas increase with time in Japanese oak casks, so a 40-year-old mizunara-aged whisky has double the incense aromas and over three times the coconut ones. Younger mizunara, however, has much more subtle and dry woody notes than the honeyed sweetness of American white oak. None of this makes mizunara better, only different. Variation in whisky gives blenders a more expressive palette, resulting in a greater array of aromas and flavors.

Left It takes mizunara trees at least 150 years to grow to a diameter that's suitable for casks.
Below Cut mizunara wood has an appealing tiger-like pattern known as *torafu* (虎斑), meaning "tiger stripes."

Making Japanese Whisky Even More Japanese

Since Japan does not have regulations about what kind of wood whisky must be aged in, coopers have a wider variety from which to choose. While American white oak dominates and *mizunara* is a pricey and tricky alternative, whisky makers have other options for creating even more distinctively Japanese whiskies. "In the past," says Ariake Barrel's Takayoshi Odawara, "we've simply made casks for whisky makers. But we've decided we need to better meet needs that distilleries didn't even know they had."

At Ariake Barrel's Kyoto headquarters, Odawara puts several vials on a hardwood table. Each is filled with amber-colored neutral spirit labeled in Japanese: *kuri* (chestnut), *sugi* (Japanese cedar) and *sakura* (cherry blossoms), which mark the wood that the alcohol was matured in. These are test samples to show what flavor profiles are possible. The concept is that distilleries can use lids, or heads, made from these woods while aging whisky in American white oak

casks, creating new and unique aromas. Each of these samples has been aged with a block of the corresponding wood for only a week to show how a neutral spirit is influenced. It's not legal to use wood chips in casks in Japan to bring out these notes, Odawara explains, which is why the decision was taken to use the casks' heads. These woods are not ideal for entire casks because they are difficult to work and might overpower the spirit, but they can bring out new and natural flavors that open up a range of Japanese possibilities.

"Here, smell this," Odawara says, handing me a vial of neutral spirit. "That's white liquor, 30 percent alcohol, and a characterless spirit." He then picks up another one, saying, "Now, try this." It smells like the chestnut cream dessert known as Mont Blanc, which makes sense because the label reads "chestnut" in Japanese. But instead of simply a nutty profile, there is a delicious sweetness. For Japanese, chestnuts evoke fall and are often mixed with rice in a dish

known as *kuri gohan* or "chestnut rice."

"Give this one a try," Odawara says, unscrewing the glass vial's metal lid. The scent is familiar to everyone in Japan. It's *sakura mochi* or cherry blossom rice cakes, which are wrapped in sakura tree leaves. Another glass vial, filled with amber spirit, is labeled *ringo* in Japanese, or "apple."

"For Scotch, you have to use oak," says Odawara, "but for Japanese whisky, you can use different kinds of woods, and we wanted to use these to produce uniquely Japanese flavors." Mission accomplished.

Above Charring a cask head that hasn't yet been circular cut.
Left Takayoshi Odawara checks a cask head at Ariake Barrel's cooperage in Miyazaki Prefecture.
Right Small bottles of spirit aged in kuri (クリ) or chestnut, sakura (サクラ) or cherry blossom wood, sugi (スギ) or Japanese cedar and mizunara (ミズナラ). The sugi and mizunara woods have been charred.

The Barrel Apprentice

Nakahama Manjiro (aka John Manjiro) was the first recorded Japanese to not only arrive in the Continental United States but also to live there where he became a Western-style barrel-making apprentice.

In 1841, 14-year-old Manjiro and a small fishing crew were shipwrecked on an island in the Pacific. This was a time when the general populous was legally not allowed to leave Japan under penalty of death. Rescued by an American whaling vessel, Manjiro was brought to Fairhaven, Massachusetts, where he learned to make casks to hold whale oil. After traveling around the world on a whaling ship, at the age of 24 Manjiro made the risky decision to return to Japan. He did, avoiding the death penalty, and he became an invaluable advisor and translator, helping to ease suspicions between the Americans and the Shogunate.

While in the United States, it's possible that Manjiro tried American whiskey but there are no historical records. (It is known that he loved coffee with loads of sugar!) According to Manjiro historian Junji Kitadai, there were also opportunities for him to have a drink with foreign merchants after returning to Japan, but again there are no records. There is one story of a British steamship anchored in Urado Bay in 1866. Manjiro told off the sailors for trespassing and they apologized, inviting Manjiro and his companion, the samurai statesman Shojiro Goto, aboard for refreshments. According to one account, Scotch was served, and Goto, who always enjoyed a good drink, tasted whisky for the first time. The account does not state whether or not Manjiro partook but it is an early account of Scotch whisky in Japan.

Here's where things get tricky and expensive. As Japan modernized, it needed more and more lumber to build and many of the biggest mizunara trees were cut down for domestic use and for export. The trees take up to 200 years to reach a size where they can be turned into prime lumber. "If the tree isn't 70–80 centimeters [27–31 in] in diameter, then it's not big enough to turn into casks," says Takayoshi Odawara, Managing Director at Ariake Barrel. Size isn't the only issue. Complicating things is the way mizunara grows. The tree's branches twist and turn, resulting in wood that's not ideal for casks. Moreover, many tall, thick mizunara trees were cut down in the late 19th and 20th century for export or to meet growing domestic demand. The difficulty in finding tall, straight Japanese oak trees makes the Chichibu Distillery's 160-cm (5.25-ft)-tall mizunara washbacks, used in fermentation, all the more remarkable.

Mizunara is hard to come by. Even Japanese whisky giant Suntory, which uses Japanese oak-aged whiskies in its Yamazaki single malts and Hibiki blends, can only get enough mizunara to make 150 casks annually. Rival Nikka might prefer American white oak but is only able to procure five or so Japanese oak casks a year. Ariake Barrel, however, produces up to around 200 mizunara casks annually. The

rarity of Japanese oak makes mizunara casks more than twice as expensive as American oak ones. Ariake Barrel, for example, sells 450-liter (119-gallon) American white oak casks for between 130,000 yen and 140,000 yen (US$1,140–$1,228 at the time of writing), but for mizunara casks the price shoots up to 320,000 yen (US$2,807) per cask.

To buy mizunara lumber, some Japanese whisky makers go to auctions in Hokkaido, where they have to compete with Japanese furniture makers and, more recently, foreign buyers. This has made an already expensive lumber even more so. According to Odawara, "The prices at auctions have gotten so high that here at Ariake Barrel we now buy direct." Palettes of Japanese oak arrive at Ariake Barrel's cooperage ready to be fashioned into casks. While furniture makers can use mizunara intended for casks, coopers are unable to use Japanese oak intended for tables, chairs and whatnot, because furniture can be made from mizunara with less than ideal grain but casks cannot. Mizunara must be cut a certain way if it's to have a second life in whisky maturation.

After Japanese oak is chopped down, the timber is split into different slices in what's called *mikanwari* or "tangerine splitting." This ensures that the wood is split with the grain and not across it. "If you don't cut it this way," says Odawara,

"you'll end up with whisky all over the floor." It's not only the way mizunara is cut, but how much is usable. About one-half of an American white oak log, minus parts like the bark and the inner core, yields enough workable wood for cask staves. "But for mizunara," he continues, "you can only use about 20–30 percent of each log." The difference is due to the character of American white oak that makes it possible to cut the log in a range of ways to make each individual panel, or stave, of the cask. American white oak can be cut across the grain because the wood naturally forms cellular growths call tyloses, which also act as natural sealants. American white oak's ability to form tyloses is one of many reasons why the wood is an ideal container for whisky. Mizunara, however, produces significantly less tyloses, meaning the wood is far more porous. "If you have ten American white oak casks and one of them leaks, that is a lot," Odawara says. "For mizunara, if you have ten casks, ten of them will eventually leak." Even if great care is taken with how the wood is cut and then split and how the cask is constructed, there are bound to be leaks in

unforeseen places. "Mizunara leaks, sure, but so does French oak," Odawara points out, adding that in years past whisky distilleries were probably more used to leaky casks than they are after switching to mainly ex-bourbon American white oak casks after World War II.

For leaky casks, Ariake Barrel has a natural solution—*kakishibu* (柿渋), or astringent persimmon juice. Throughout Japanese history, kakishibu has been used as a natural sealant. In sake production, wooden lids, Japanese-style casks and tubs are waterproofed with the juice. The entire mizunara cask isn't covered in kakishibu, just the leaky spots, allowing the cask to continue to breath and interact with the spirit throughout maturation.

Mizunara might not suit every Japanese whisky. It's expensive, tricky and requires a constant eye. In short, mizunara is a massive pain in the ass. Yet, it can produce a beautifully strong yet subtle whisky that holds up brilliantly in blends. The attention that's required to make these precious mizunara casks and then the care necessary for proper aging might cause some distilleries to throw their hands up in frustration. The word that comes to mind is *gaman* (我慢), which is translated as "patience," "endurance" or even "self-control." This isn't just a word but a Buddhist philosophy, and to make mizunara casks and mizunara-aged whisky requires loads of gaman—not to mention lots of money!

Right Suntory began aging its whisky in mizunara casks during World War II. Today, mizunara-aged whiskies are integrale to Suntory's single malts and blends.
Below A mizunara cask at the Nagahama Distillery.

Above left Chichibu cooper Kenta Nagae splits a mizunara log.
Above center The dark brown section on this mizunara cask has been covered with kakishibu.
Above right While Ariake Barrel believes kakishibu helps prevent leakage, the Chichibu Distillery tries to split the wood by axe so that the distilled spirit stays in the cask. At Ariake Barrel, the mizunara arrives pre-cut on pallets.

Japan's Whisky Drinking Culture

When Shirofuda, Japan's first whisky, was released in 1929, Japanese customers turned their nose up at its smoky drams, saying the tipple smelt burnt and stinky. Japanese people simply weren't used to drinking alcohol that strong, and whisky overpowered both sake and shochu. Today, many Japanese whisky drinkers and distillers love the smokiest Scotch whiskies, but considering how subtle the aromas are in Japanese cooking, it took time for the country to warm up to whisky.

The Highball

Soda, ice and whisky. This is the most common way whisky is enjoyed across the country. The drink has a long history in Japan, and the way it's enjoyed has changed over the years. Bar Samboa, which opened in Kobe in 1918, still serves what's closest to the pre-World War II highball—whisky, soda, a twist of lemon and no ice.

The first hit among Japanese whisky, Suntory Whisky 12 year, was ideal for highballs. Released in 1937 when Kotobukiya wasn't yet officially called Suntory, this blend's

softer, floral notes were popular with customers who referred to this whisky as *kakubin*, or "square bottle." The name stuck. Today, the official name is "Kakubin Whisky" and it's the most common mixer for highballs, even having its own moniker, "Kaku Hai" (角ハイ).

When whisky first started to reach a mass Japanese public in the 1930s, the whisky was cut with water (*mizuwari*) or with carbonated water (*sodawari*). This hasn't changed much, and these, along with "on the rocks," are still the most common ways whisky is served. During the 1960s, Suntory

42

promoted its Torys whisky as a hot beverage a la shochu in a style known as *oyuwari* (cut with hot water). Sake is also enjoyed hot, but even in chilly weather the Japanese today generally do not drink their whisky hot. These days, however, some Japanese distilleries, like Chichibu, design their whiskies to be served neat.

In the early 1960s, Suntory made drinking highballs even easier by putting them in cans so that folks could guzzle them on the bullet train or while out picnicking during that decade's big camping boom. Blends and soda brought whisky to a larger audience, just as they did in the late 19th century when the English shifted from brandy to whisky.

When the country's whisky business was at historic lows in the 2000s, it was Kakubin that led the highball resurgence with a series of commercials in 2008 featuring the actress Koyuki of *The Last Samurai* fame. Young Japanese women who had never shown any interest in whisky were suddenly drinking highballs made at the standard three parts carbonated water, one part Kakubin. The same whisky that made the Japanese whisky industry helped its comeback.

Top A Torys Bar in Shinjuku, circa 1954. During their peak, there were over 2,000 Torys Bars. Today, only a few remain. One of the most iconic, Juso Torys Bar, was destroyed by fire in 2014 but thankfully has since been rebuilt.

Above As Chris Bunting's book *Drinking Japan* points out, Japan is truly the best place to drink alcohol in the world.

Far left Dapper bartenders serve customers at a Torys Bar in 1955.

Left Bartender Makoto Ono at the excellent Cordon Noir in Kyoto showing off a sherry cask Yamazaki.

Below When it launched, Torys was promoted as "cheap" (やすい or *yasui*) and "delicious" (うまい or *umai*).

Crafting a Very Japanese Cocktail

"When appropriate, I want to put Japanese culture in the drinks I make," says bartender Ryu Fujii. For this cocktail, it is very, very appropriate. Working at Bar K in Osaka, Fujii is one of the best young bartenders in the world, representing Japan as a finalist at the 2016 Diageo World Class bartending competition. One of his signature drinks is an original cocktail called "Japonism," based on an idea from his mentor, former K's bartender Shuichi Tanaka. "Here, original cocktails like this have been relatively rare," Fujii says, explaining that most bartenders in Japan tend to prefer to perfect or tweak existing recipes. You want an amazing Manhattan? Order one in Japan. However, like Fujii, there are more and more Japanese bartenders breaking new ground with original creations.

"With this cocktail, the goal was to bring out the deep flavor of Yamazaki but not harm the subtleness of the whisky's boutique," Fujii says. All of the cocktail's ingredients do exactly that. Japonism is made with *hojicha* (roasted green tea), brown syrup, a dash of orange bitters and a shot of Yamazaki 12. Spooning hojicha into a teapot, Fujii adds, "I use *matcha* for cocktails made from white liquor, but for brown spirits hojicha is best." Matcha has bitter notes that don't work as well with the caramel flavors found in hojicha.

Fujii takes a butane lighter to *hinoki* (Japanese cypress) shavings, sending them up in the flames and then snuffing them out with a glass. The aromatic hinoki is used to make

"Most Japanese bars don't have original cocktails," says award-winning bartender Ryu Fujii as he makes his signature Japonism. "They instead prefer to improve on existing ones, like the Manhattan."

Anti-clockwise from top left First, hojicha is brewed. Fuji takes a butane lighter to Japanese cypress shavings. Then he smokes the glass. After mixing the hojicha with Yamazaki 12 year, a dark sugary syrup called *kuromitsu* (literally, "black honey"), and orange bitters, the cocktail is strained into the ice-filled smoked glass. Here, ice cubes are used instead of an ice sphere because they help lift out the cocktail's aromas. Finally, Japonism is served with an orange slice.

Left Ice spheres can give whisky a Japanese spin. Unlike cubes, the round spheres keep their cool longer and melt more slowly. Each sphere is hand carved from an ice block (Fujii uses a three-pronged Japanese ice pick) and then refrozen for hardening. Before serving, the spheres get touch-up carvings and a quick cold water wash to smooth out the surface.

everything from traditional Japanese bathtubs to temple and shrine structures. He mixes the Yamazaki, the hojicha, brown syrup and bitters with ice cubes before pouring the drink into the smoke glass and serving with a slice of orange. The resulting cocktail evokes memories of incense-filled Japanese temples in summer to chilly mandarian groves in winter, with breezes of delicate floral spring and rich autumn leaves. Japonism encapsulates the country's seasons like few cocktails can.

marketing campaign at home linking its whisky to traditional Japanese food. But in real world Japan, do people really drink whisky with their meals? They sure do. But it's important to think about how alcohol and food are consumed in the country.

Beer rules the roost, outselling sake, shochu and whisky. It still remains the default drink, which is why when people go out in groups, whether with co-workers or customers, the first round is typically, but not always, beer before moving on to other drinks. There is even an expression for this, *toriaezu biiru*, "Let's start with beer." Beer is a way to begin the evening with something everyone generally likes and to ensure everyone kicks off the dining experience together. Japanese beer tends to be relatively light and unobtrusive on the eating experience, just as sake and shochu do not detract from the meal. "The problem with straight whisky is that the cask influence can overwhelm a traditional Japanese meal," says bartender Ryu Fujii (see pages 44–45). "That's why, as much as I love whisky, I'd honestly recommend sake."

Since Japanese highballs have such a high carbonated concentration compared to whisky (3:1), this helps explain why the fizzy drink works better with food than whisky served neat. Adding soda or water brings whisky's high alcohol down so that it doesn't detract from the meal and is in line with other Japanese drinks such as sake, which is usually bottled at between 14 and 20 percent alcohol by volume, or shochu, which is typically around 25 percent abv, or even beer. Suntory promotes its highballs as fitting companions for *karaage* or Japanese fried chicken because whisky with soda goes well with greasy Japanese soul food. "Don't think that any Japanese whisky served straight will go with any kind of Japanese meal," says Teruhiko Yamamoto of Bar Keith in Osaka. "There will be things that clash, so depending on what you're eating, sake still might be a better choice." At his bar, Yamamoto has organized special tastings and pairings with Japanese food and *wagashi* (Japanese sweets) but believes that a lot of thought must go into such pairings. He also thinks that entirely new dishes should be created with whisky in mind.

In Japan, bars are still the place where aficionados go, and since many of these establishments also serve Scotch, Irish

Top Highballs are often served with Japanese soul food, such as the Osaka favorite takoyaki (squid tentacles in fried batter served with a savory sauce, mayo, dried skipjack tuna shavings and green onions).
Above In Tokyo, takoyaki is seen as a snack. In Osaka, it's considered a meal.

Japanese Whisky and Food

The idea that Japanese whisky goes with Japanese food isn't new. During the mid-1960s, Suntory tried to tell Americans just that with newspaper ads stating "Sushi Sashimi Sukiyaki Suntory." The following decade, Suntory launched a and American whiskies, the decor is often Western influenced, as is the food. Typically, the focus is the whisky itself or cocktails, and any eats that are served might be small snacks, with sausages, nuts, cheeses and chocolate being the default, or dried squid for a more local flavor. Western food

or *yoshoku*, such as pasta or pizza, is also common. So don't feel that Japanese whisky must be eaten with Japanese food, because even in Japan it's not. Saying that Japanese whisky is specifically designed to go with Japanese food seems like marketing spin, especially after Suntory bought Jim Beam in 2014 and Jim Beam highballs, called *biimu hai* (ビームハイ), have started showing up in Japanese pubs! Honestly, nearly any decent to good whisky, whether it's Japanese, American, Canadian or Scotch, that's mixed with lots of soda will suit *most* Japanese cuisine just fine.

Eating Japanese food, however, certainly impacts how whisky is blended in Japan and how the Japanese taste certain flavors in the whisky when they are not enjoying whisky with food. The biggest influence, perhaps, is a steady diet of rice. Not all rice in Japan is the same. There are different varieties that can be polished to different levels before being washed, cooked and eaten, thereby changing the character and flavor. Other subtleties that people also notice include when the rice was harvested. It's not that the Japanese have better palettes, but the country's cuisine certainly does foster one.

For those looking for ideal Japanese whiskies to enjoy as highballs with food, Suntory's Kakubin, non-age Hakushu and Hibiki are recommended, as is Nikka's Black, Clear and Rich Blend. White Oak's and Mars Whisky's blends also work well. But honestly, Japan might be fussy about the correct way to eat sushi, the proper way to hold chopsticks and how to take a bath, but there is no best way to enjoy Japanese whisky and no best Japanese dishes to enjoy with it. There are ways you like best, so experiment and explore.

Above Highballs pair well with *tempura* because they complement the dish's crispy fried batter.
Left Japanese whisky surrounded by signs for Western-style olives, goat cheese and pickled dishes.

What Makes Japanese Whisky "Japanese"?

To truly understand Japanese whisky, you must understand Japanese culture. The country's whisky tradition is a reflection of everything from national identity and industrialization to art and even religion. It's more than just a drink, it's the spirit of modern Japan. Japanese whisky is also defined in several ways.

Balance

One defining characteristic is that Japanese whisky is cultural. Japanese writing puts great emphasis on balance, and children starting in grade school spend hours writing increasingly complicated *kanji* characters. Teachers go through with red pens, nixing characters that are noticeably lopsided or even just barely. Much of the Japanese attention to detail has its roots in its written language, which forces individuals to notice variations, sometimes small and sometimes large, between similar-looking written characters.

Japanese calligraphy, called *shodo*, shows how expressive the language can be. It's no accident that numerous Japanese whisky labels, taking their cue from sake and *shochu* bottles,

are covered in shodo. This is not simply because it's an easy way to brand Japanese whisky, but as a form of artistic expression it also provides insight into the national psyche. Not every Japanese whisky label features calligraphy, but since the early 1960s it's become a signifier of the country's amber liquid. Even if the spirit the bottle contains isn't perfectly balanced, the kanji calligraphy that cover bottles of Japanese whisky signifies this desire for balance.

"Balance" doesn't mean "meek," "careful" or even "neat." Again, look at Japanese calligraphy. Shodo can express passion and emotion, just as whisky can. But even the most dynamic Japanese calligraphy balances the characters so that the writing doesn't appear lopsided. The same goes for

Bar Cordon Noir in Kyoto has over 1,000 bottles of whisky, including Scotch, bourbon, Irish and Japanese. Each type is a reflection of the culture and tradition in which it was created. To fully understand each type, it's necessary to know its history and its language.

the most robust Japanese whiskies, like Karuizawa, giving them greater depth, complexity and nuance.

When talking about balance in Japanese whisky, a good place to look is *washoku*, or Japanese food, namely the thought behind it. Traditional Japanese food is arranged so that it is offset by flavor and color. Each small dish complements the whole but does not detract from it. When you eat washoku, you are supposed to eat from the different dishes at the same pace so that you finish them all roughly at the same time for a totality of taste. Eating all your rice, gulping down all your *miso* soup and then moving on to a side of vegetables is bad manners, and children are admonished for this. Because of this eating style, in which the goal is to finish all the different little dishes at the same time, the Japanese experience their meals in a balanced way, which perhaps subconsciously influences other aspects of their life. Work? Not so much. Whisky? Most certainly.

This could be why many, but by not means all, Japanese whiskies are often well balanced. There are exceptions, of course, but often with many Japanese whiskies nothing overwhelms and detracts, with different notes counteracted by other flavors, with each part of the whisky coming together in concert for an overall experience.

Flexibility

Since Japan doesn't have a whisky-trading tradition, distilleries must be incredibly versatile. "Relations are good within the Scotch whisky industry, but when talking about Japan we're on bad terms with Nikka, so it's not like we're going to do something together," says Suntory chief blender Shinji Fukuyo. Individual distillers and blenders may get along fine with those at rival makers (and they seem to!), but the current corporate culture of these whisky giants puts them at loggerheads. That's why if Nikka or Suntory need something, they'll make it in-house. This is also why some Japanese distilleries, such as Yamazaki, have a hodgepodge of pot stills, because different shapes impact the types of whiskies they make, whether that's distilling heavy, even oily spirits or much lighter ones. Not only are the shapes different but Suntory heats the stills by varied methods—some by gas flame, while others are indirectly heated by steam—both of which impart different characteristics to the distilled spirit. This also means it's possible to make a wide variety of whiskies.

Having multiple distilleries means Japanese whisky makers can swap stock within their own companies so they don't have to trade with outsiders. Not only does this integrated production model mean greater flexibility but also total control over production. Even Mars Whisky, a smaller whisky maker with a rich history, opened a second distillery in the fall of 2016 that produces a different style of whisky, allowing the ability to tailor-make blends to exact specifications. The other variations for Japanese whisky makers include different yeast strains and on-site cooperages that not only refurbish and repair casks but make brand-new ones, giving the distillery greater control over their production and their ability to make changes.

One of the biggest ways in which Japanese whisky is flexible stems from the country's laws regarding whisky—or, rather, the comparative lack of them. "There are regulations regarding whisky in Japan," Nikka's chief blender Tadashi Sakuma says, "but they're lax." For example, unlike in the US and the UK there is no legal minimum period of matura-

tion, there are no rules about what kinds of wood must be used in maturation, and whisky in Japan doesn't have the same minimum alcohol percentage requirements that, say, Scotch does. "There is no legal definition of Japanese whisky," says Suntory's chief blender Shinji Fukuyo. "I think it might be good to have a legal definition of Japanese whisky, because when asked what it was, it would be easy to explain. However, if that definition became so strictly defined, like with Scotch, then we'd lose all the flexibility we have."

In Scotland, for example, whisky must be aged in oak for at least three years and bottled at 40 percent alcohol, while in the United States bourbon whiskey, for example, must contain at least 51 percent corn as well as be aged in charred, virgin white oaks casks. Further, it must not contain colorants and must be bottled at 40 percent alcohol. Japan has no detailed regulations of this sort. The definition of whisky itself isn't as rigid, because in Japan it can be bottled at 37 percent or 39 percent alcohol and still be called whisky. Bottling at a lower alcohol percentage is one way Japanese makers skirt around paying higher taxes, especially on the cheap stuff. In short, distilleries can pretty much slap "whisky" on a bottle and that's exactly what they've got, "whisky." Or, at least, *uisukii*.

"The whisky we export to Europe, for example, adheres to European regulations. The whisky that we only

Below Suntory Old was originally supposed to be released in 1940 but was delayed until 1950 because of World War II. In 1961, the label for Suntory Old's US release featured Shinjiro Torii's *kotobuki* (寿) calligraphy, the first time kanji brushwork was used on a proper whisky label. The English words "Japanese Whisky" were another first.

Above A poster from 1950 featuring the red Japanese sun. The text at the top reads "Peaceful Japan Banzai," while the small print next to the black oval at the bottom suggests flying the Japanese flag on national holidays.
Right Officially known as Suntory Whisky, Shirofuda's label showed a red sun against a white background, clearly evocative of the Japanese national flag.

Above On November 11 every year, Yamazaki Distillery workers gather at Shiio Shrine to honor the day the distillery's still was first fired up. The characters on the side of the shrine's wrapping read "Dedicated to Shinjiro Torii."
Above left Cask staves burn as Shinto priests enter the shrine.

Above On the left is a *miko*, or "shrine maiden," while Yamazaki whisky casks flank the main altar. Behind them are sake cask offerings.
Right A Yamazaki worker tends to a fire in front of the shrine. Cask staves are ritually burned.

sell domestically doesn't need to follow those rules because it's not for export," says Nikka's chief blender Tadashi Sakuma. Nikka is not alone, and other award-winning Japanese whisky makers do the exact same thing. However, those pricey Japanese single malts and blends that collect awards and accolades do conform to internationally agreed-upon whisky standards regarding age statements and maturation lengths. It's often the inexpensive whiskies sold in enormous plastic bottles that might not as they are not intended for export.

Despite any differences that Suntory and Nikka have, both view the flexibility Japanese whisky has as a vital asset. Because of this rather nebulous framework, Japanese whisky making has greater room to play than its Scottish and American brethren. "Perhaps because the thinking is more flexible in Japan about what whisky is and because we don't have all these rules and pre-set notions, we are freed up and able to try new things," says Nikka's Tadashi Sakuma. "I don't think there's a reason to change current Japanese regulations for whisky."

The lack of iron-clad rules but the awareness of and respect for tradition, frees up the Japanese approach to whisky making. "When I was working in Scotland, I'd sometimes suggest certain changes to their process like we do in Japan," recalls Yoichi Distillery manager Koichi Nishikawa, who previously headed up the Nikka-owned Ben Nevis Distillery. "The reaction tended to be, 'Well, that is Japan and this is Scotland.'"

The Spirit of Japan

One of the most important concepts to keep in mind when discussing Japanese whisky is *wakon yosai* (和魂洋才), with *wakon* (和魂) meaning "Japanese spirit" and *yosai* (洋才) referring to "Western technology." This isn't the spirit that's typically mentioned around distilleries, but the soul and the heartbeat. The phrase wakon yosai appeared in the late 19th century in Japan as the country was making its big push to

This Suntory whisky crest is clearly British-influenced, but Suntory workers don't refer to the animals on either side as "standing lions," but rather as *shishi*, mythical creatures that ward off evil.

modernize, but it wasn't a new concept. It's an updating of the older *wakon kansai* (和魂漢才) or "Japanese spirit, Chinese learning," when Japan, for well over a thousand years, took what it needed from China, such as writing and Buddhism, but tweaked and made it its own. The idea is that if the Japanese applied Western techniques, they would do it their way because the Japanese are never content to take things as they are. Inevitably, they will add their own spin and improve things when necessary. The result will be different. Japanese whisky is proof of that.

From the birth of Japanese whisky, when the first bottles were carried out of the Yamazaki Distillery in 1929, those distillery workers knew that they were making a Japanese product. Even if the labels were almost entirely in English, no doubt to meet people's preconceived notions, the first proper Japanese whisky ever made, Suntory Whisky or Shirofuda (White Label), had a Japanese sensibility. The label featured a white background, hence the White Label moniker, and a red dot. In Japan, the sun is not traditionally portrayed in yellow or orange as in the West. It's red. Japan's indigenous religion, Shintoism, is centered around the sun. And yet, here on the bottle, we have the sun. Not only that, it's presented against a white background, turning Shirofuda into a national flag. In Japanese, the country is 日本 (Nihon or Nippon) and those characters literally mean "the origin of the sun." The name Suntory itself is also a direct allusion to the sun, to Shinto gates and to its founder Shinjiro Torii. While Shirofuda was a flop, the second whisky that Torii and Co. followed up with, Akafuda (Red Label), once again showed an acute awareness that the distillery was making Japanese whisky. White and red are the two most important colors in Japanese culture. They are also the colors of the country's first two proper whiskies. From the get go, Japanese whisky makers were aware they were making Japanese whisky.

same decade, a bottle would pop up in the James Bond film *You Only Live Twice*. The original book contains several mentions of Suntory whisky, and while Bond author and Scotsman Ian Fleming thought it was "very good," Bond turned his nose up at it, preferring sake or his standard martini. His loss!

Whisky of the Gods

Centered around nature and notions of purity, Shintoism is Japan's indigenous religion. There are an estimated 100,000 Shinto shrines dotting the country, housing deities known as *kami* and protecting the surrounding areas in which they're located. It's only natural for Japanese whisky makers to feel connected to Japanese religion. Even today, it's not unusual for Japanese distilleries to have Shinto priests bless their equipment, whether it be the forklifts or the pot stills. Inside the Chichibu Distillery, there's a portable Shinto altar known as a *kamidana*, common at sake breweries, while every morning at the Mars Whisky Shinshu Distillery workers gather at a small Shinto shrine on the distillery grounds to pray. Shinto garlands adorn Nikka's pot stills at both Yoichi and Miyagikyo, and Suntory's Chita Distillery has a *torii* (gate) and a small Shinto shrine out front.

Sake brewers have a close relationship to Shintoism because purity is important for both the religion and the drink. The first mention of sake appeared in the 8th-century text *The Kojiki* (The Record of Ancient Matters), the earliest account of Japanese history, with the gods getting together to knock back some booze. One of Kyoto's oldest Shinto shrines, Matsunoo Taisha, established in 701, has a long association with sake brewing. Today, sake makers continue to make the pilgrimage to Matsunoo Taisha, as do an increasing number of Japanese whisky distillers, underscoring a natural connection between Shintoism and the liquor. For those who can't make the trip, they can always visit one of the 100,000 Shinto shrines in Japan. This is why the shrines near Japanese distilleries are important. Distillers pray not only for good whisky but also ask for safety and protection for their workers and their distillery.

This connection between Japanese whisky and the spiritual world is not new. From the very start of Japanese whisky, there's been Japanese religion. Behind Suntory's Yamazaki Distillery sits a Shinto shrine called Shiio Shrine. Founded in 746, the shrine was originally a Buddhist temple but changed to a shrine during the Meiji Restoration when

Shishi exist in pairs, with two stone statues standing in front of Buddhist temples and Shinto shrines, just as two appear on the Suntory crest. Shishi are translated in English as "guardian lions" or "guardian dogs."

When Suntory Old first went on sale in Japan in 1950, for example, the label stated in rather awkward English "Produce of Japan." Later, in 1962, when Suntory Old launched in the United States, its label proudly read "Japanese Whisky," marking the first time a Japanese whisky was marketed as such. (It also added that it was distilled "near Kyoto," perhaps because that sounded more picturesque than "in Osaka.") The bottle featured the kanji character 寿 (*kotobuki*, meaning both "longevity" and "congratulations"), a nod to Suntory's then corporate name, Kotobukiya.

Around that same time, billboards went up in the US showing a Japanese woman in a kimono offering Suntory Old and a tagline that read "Discovery Suntory The Classic Whisky from Japan." It wasn't cheap, with a bottle priced at US$7.25, the same as Johnnie Walker Red. Later that

Buddhism and Shintoism were forcibly separated. Buddhist temples were converted to Shinto shrines and Buddhist priests were defrocked, all to strengthen the Emperor and what became a national Shinto religion. Today, both Buddhism and Shintoism have returned to their peaceful co-existence, with the majority of Japanese believing in both. Shiio Shrine houses three deities, including Susanoo, the god of the sea and storms, Emperor Shomu, who reigned in the 8th century, and Emperor Go-Toba, who reigned in the late 12th century. On the grounds other deities are housed in smaller shrines, including the sun goddess Amaterasu, the deity from which all Japanese emperors are said to descend.

Each year on November 11 at 11:11 am, this shrine neighboring the Yamazaki Distillery holds a fall festival for Suntory founder Shinjiro Torii (for more, see page 51). At exactly 11.11 am, a ceremony commences, with Suntory workers gathering to celebrate, pay their respects and pray. In Japanese, the 11/11 is an example of *zorome* (ぞろ目) or when the same numbers line up. The date also marks when the distillery was finished in 1924 and, according to Suntory lore, at 11.11 am and 11 seconds the stills started up. In front of sake barrels, whisky cask offerings sit on either side of the main shrine's inner altar, and a Shinto priest says prayers.

Distillery workers gather outside, while locals and those connected to Suntory sit inside the shrine during the ritual. The close association with this shrine could be why Suntory calls the two animals flanking the crest on its pot stills *shishi* and not simply lions (ライオン; *raion* is Japanese for "lion"). Shishi are mythical creatures that stand guard at Shinto shrines and Buddhist temples to ward off evil. At Shiio Shrine, two shishi flank each side of the main shrine's walkway, just as they stand guard on the stills.

Shintoism doesn't have a doctrine, biblical text or rules to follow as in Western religions but it does have myths, as collected in *The Kojiki*. Shrines dot mountains to protect local areas, and festivals and shrine rites are held to appease the deities or kami and ask for protection. For most Japanese, when babies are born they are blessed at Shinto shrines but when people die a Buddhist priest typically handles the funeral rites. The reason is that Shintoism is concerned with purity and cleanliness whereas death is a dirty business. The obsession with cleanliness is why people wash their hands (and even clean out their mouths) when visiting Shinto shrines, also striking at the heart of Japan's bathing culture. Moreover, it explains why clear sake is used in Shinto ceremonies. Since sake is made from rice, and Shinto

Made from hemp or rice straw, a shimenawa hangs across Shiio Shrine's torii gate, marking the shrine as a sacred place. The white zig-zag streamers are called *shide* and are used in purification rituals. Originally, this torii gate was located at the opposite end of the street, meaning that Yamazaki Distillery workers passed under it on their way to work. Decades ago, it's said that the gate was moved near the shrine so that trucks could easy get up and down the street.

is connected to nature and the harvest, it is the soul of Japan. It is why the mythic quality water is sometimes given in whisky making and the emphasis on purity have been so appealing to Japanese distillers over the years. This helped whisky feel more familiar and, ultimately, more Japanese.

Since Japanese whisky is part of Japanese life, Shinto rituals are naturally performed at distilleries. At Nikka's Yoichi Distillery, Shinto garlands called *shimenawa* adorn the pot stills, protecting them against evil, and every January, after the New Year's holidays have finished and the Yoichi employees return to work, a Shinto priest blesses the stills. Safety is taken with the utmost seriousness, so consider these blessings added insurance, because in the 1940s there was a still house fire. The shimenawa have another function. They mark a *yorishiro*, which is, essentially, a landing pad for kami or Shinto deities. Yorishiro are typically long, thin or cylindrical objects, such as tree trunks. Another Shinto garland hangs in the entryway of the Yoichi Distillery's first maturation warehouse to mark the spot as sacred.

Shintoism, however, is not a demanding religion, nor does it prohibit believers from following other religious beliefs

Shinto garlands called shimenawa hang around the necks of the pot stills at Yoichi Distillery. The reason for the variation between the two stills is that Miyake Industries refurbished the one on the left in late 2015, explaining why the base is shinier. When stills are refurbished, the replacements are made to the exact specifications of the previous still in order not to change the character of the spirit.

and practices, such as Buddhism, that co-exist. Keizo Saji, the former Suntory president responsible for launching the Yamazaki single malt, was a devout Buddhist, but like most Japanese he also believed in Shintoism. The two beliefs are not mutually exclusive. This is why most Japanese are Shinto *and* Buddhist, with each religion serving a different function. However, Shinto thinking and beliefs are so ingrained in Japanese culture, it's difficult, if not impossible, to separate the two. The same is true of Japan and its whisky.

So, what exactly is Japanese whisky? Is it a balanced whisky? Does it reference Japanese culture? Does it need to be 100 percent Japanese? The best definition is perhaps from the Chichibu Distillery founder Ichiro Akuto: "Japanese whisky is whisky made by Japanese people."

Japan's Leading Distilleries and Whiskies

It's an exciting time to be a Japanese whisky fan. The upside is that the country is making truly great whisky, wowing folks all over the world. The downside is that getting coveted blends and single malts is harder than ever! The good news is that more Japanese whisky is coming. Starting in 2016, a handful of new Japanese distilleries were established, the most promising of which are covered in the Afterword. They're still finding their footing and their best whiskies are still a few years off, so it's too soon to put them up there with Japan's world-class distilleries. The early indications, however, are promising.

This book and the map below do not profile Japanese whisky makers who, as of writing, aren't distilling domestically and are simply aging and bottling imported Scotch. Ditto for those not making whisky from traditional grains like barley, corn and rye. While this book doesn't contain a list of bars or pubs (see Tuttle's *Drinking Japan* for that), it does have a look at today's leading Japanese distilleries and the whiskies they've made. The context and culture behind the drinks make it easier to appreciate that next dram or bottle.

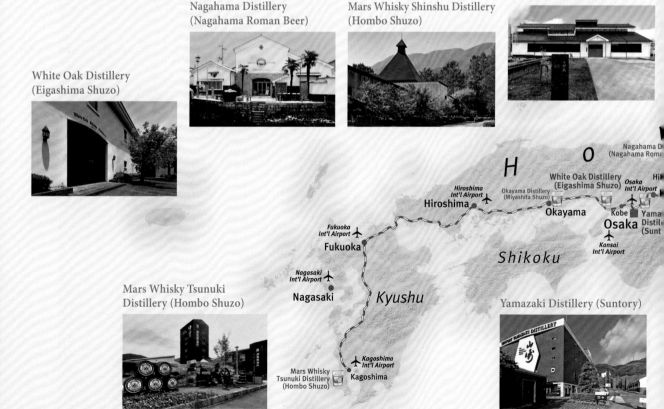

Saburomaru Distillery
(Wakatsuru Shuzo)

Nagahama Distillery
(Nagahama Roman Beer)

Mars Whisky Shinshu Distillery
(Hombo Shuzo)

White Oak Distillery
(Eigashima Shuzo)

Mars Whisky Tsunuki
Distillery (Hombo Shuzo)

Yamazaki Distillery (Suntory)

Nagahama D
(Nagahama Roma

White Oak Distillery
(Eigashima Shuzo)

Okayama Distillery
(Miyashita Shuzo)

Osaka
Int'l Airport

Hi

Hiroshima
Int'l Airport

Hiroshima

Okayama

Kobe

Osaka

Yama
Distil
(Sunt

Kansai
Int'l Airport

H   O

Shikoku

Fukuoka
Int'l Airport

Fukuoka

Nagasaki
Int'l Airport

Nagasaki

Kyushu

Kagoshima
Int'l Airport

Mars Whisky
Tsunuki Distillery
(Hombo Shuzo)

Kagoshima

Japan

100 km
40 miles

N

Yoichi Distillery (Nikka)

Hokkaido

Yoichi Distillery (Nikka)   Otaru
● Sapporo
✈ New Chitose Int'l Airport

Akkeshi Distillery (Kenten)
● Kushiro

Akkeshi Distillery (Kenten)

● Aomori

Miyagikyo Distillery (Nikka)

Asaka Distillery (Sasanokawa Shuzo)

Niigata
✈ Niigata Int'l Airport

Miyagikyo Distillery (Nikka)
● Sendai
✈ Sendai Int'l Airport

Koriyama

Asaka Distillery (Sasanokawa Shuzo)

Nukuda Distillery (Kiuchi Brewery)

Chichibu Distillery (Venture Whisky)

H o n s h u

Nukuda Distillery (Kiuchi Brewery)

tillery huzo)

Mars Whisky nshu Distillery Hombo Shuzo)

Takasaki
Chichibu Distillery (Venture Whisky)

● Mito

Hakushu Distillery (Suntory)
Ina

akatsugawa
agoya
Shizuoka Distillery (Gaiaflow)

TOKYO
✈ Narita Int'l Airport
✈ Haneda Int'l Airport

Hakushu Distillery (Suntory)

Sun Grain Chita Distillery (Suntory)

Kirin Distillery Fuji Gotemba Distillery (Kirin)

● Atami

● Shizuoka

Izu Peninsula

u air ort

Kirin Distillery Fuji Gotemba Distillery (Kirin)

Sun Grain Chita Distillery (Suntory)

Shizuoka Distillery (Gaiaflow)

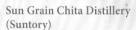

SUNTORY
YAMAZAKI DISTILLERY

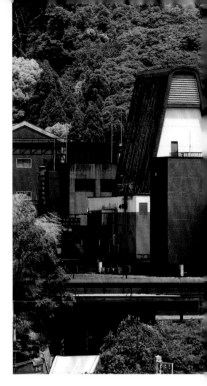

A public road cuts through the Yamazaki Distillery. Cars and scooters pass by while kids in yellow grade-school caps lug leather backpacks as they walk to class. In the nearby parking lot, buses stop and tourists file out into a small welcoming garden. Every flower is labeled—which isn't uncommon in Japan—but Suntory has gone the extra mile by including the months when they bloom. Today, it's early summer, but not yet hot, and there isn't a cloud in the sky.

"Good morning," Toshikazu Kimura says in English to a group of tourists. Kimura has been at Suntory for over 30 years. Previously the distillery manager at Suntory's Hakushu Distillery, Kimura now guides visitors through Yamazaki, offering his knowledge and expertise. He turns and says in Japanese, "We're grateful for all the international acclaim our whiskies have been getting." For Suntory, there's no shortage of that.

Crossing the street to the distillery's other side, Kimura says to watch out for cars. Traffic is sporadic but this is a public road and we are jaywalking. In front of the gift shop sits a large still that's a little over 5 meters (16 ft) high. On the neck it reads "Watanabe Iron Works Osaka." Kimura is quick to point out that this is the first still ever used at Yamazaki. To get it in the distillery in 1924, the still was put

on a boat and transported up the Yodo River, which flows along Umeda, one of Osaka City's biggest urban hubs. That was the easy part compared to getting the two-ton still across the train tracks in front of the distillery. Unsure how long it would take, the story goes that the still was pushed across the tracks at night when the trains weren't running.

Made of copper, the pot still has now greened after being left outside. Cast iron can also be used for pot stills, and often is for *shochu* stills, but in whisky making copper is ideal and for good reason. During chemical reactions, the distillate reacts with the pot still's copper, creating a more flavorful spirit. "This still was used for about 30 years, before being replaced," Kimura says, "because the copper had weakened."

Top The Yamazaki Distillery sits at the foot of Mt Tenno.
Above Suntory Kakubin is Japan's longest-selling whisky. Its bottle features a tortoise shell (亀甲 or *kikko*) pattern, which symbolizes longevity and good fortune.
Left Statues of Shinjiro Torii and his middle son Keizo Saji, who was adopted by his mother's family for inheritance reasons, a practice that was not unusual at that time. Saji, however, ended up taking over his father's business.

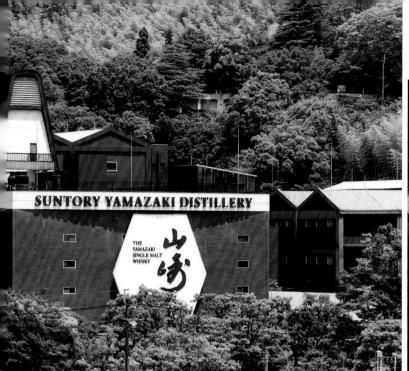

The Giants of Yamazaki

"This is Shinjiro Torii," Kimura says, pointing at one of the two statues next to the green still. "His dream was to make whisky in Japan." Born in Osaka in 1879, at 13 years of age Torii earned an apprenticeship at his uncle's business, Konishi-ya (the present-day Konishi Co. Ltd), then a pharmaceutical company but now Japan's most famous glue maker. At that time, drug companies were active in the drinks business because their knowledge of chemistry came in handy with concocting beverages. Since the late 1880s, Konishi had been making and selling "whisky." It also produced brewed beer that was bottled as Asahi and churned out Akamon Jirushi ("Red Gate Mark") wine, fizzy soft drinks and condensed milk.

By the age of 18 Torii knew enough about the beverage trade to set up his first shop, Torii Shoten, in 1899. This was the start of the company that would one day become Suntory and is why older bottles of Suntory whisky sometimes read "Since 1899." By 1906

Torii was specializing in *yoshu* or Western liquor (for more on yoshu, see pages 17–19). Known as "the nose" for his superb olfactory ability, Torii proved especially skilled at catering to the Japanese market.

The following year, Torii released his first smash hit—Akadama Port Wine. He was already importing Spanish wine but felt that Japanese consumers might prefer something sweeter, so he came up with his own blend. At that

Top Under Keizo Saji, Kotobukiya became Suntory, the Hakushu Distillery was founded and the now iconic Yamazaki and Hakushu single malts debuted as well as Hibiki.
Above Yamazaki's first still has been put out to pasture right across from the distillery's gift shop.

Above Before Kotobukiya began making real Yamazaki whisky, it had Hermes. Kotobukiya trademarked this brand in 1911, and the Hermes Old Scotch bottle above dates from that period. Tellingly, Hermes' labels listed the "Hermes Whisky Distillery" instead of Kotobukiya, and featured a "S. T. Hermes & Co." signature. Was the S. T. short for Shinjiro Torii?

Below Akadama's risqué poster caused a scandal in 1922 for showing so much skin.

Below center A 1929 Shirofuda poster reads "Wake up people!" adding that "The age of blindly accepting foreign imports is over" because Japan now has a prime domestic whisky.

Below right Launched in 1937, Kakubin is Japan's longest-selling whisky.

time the Japanese palette was slightly sweeter than it is today and people simply weren't used to wine's bitter tannins. From early on, Torii showed a flair for marketing, something that Suntory continues to excel at, and a risqué poster helped arouse interest. By the early 1920s Akadama dominated domestic wine sales, occupying more than half of the market. Torii's success in the wine business made the Yamazaki Distillery possible, and Akadama, which is still on sale in Japan, was a sign of things to come.

"The bottle featured the sun, so even then, before the company was named Suntory, there was already that connection," Kimura points out. The name Akadama literally means "red ball" and referred directly to the sun, just like on the nation's flag (in Japan, the sun is traditionally portrayed in red and not orange or yellow as in the West). Suntory is a play on words. "Sun" refers to, of course, the sun, while "tory" is a reference to both the Shinto gates, *torii*

(鳥居) in Japanese, and Shinjiro Torii's last name, which is written as 鳥井 in Japanese. Among locals in Yamazaki, there is another story that the name "Suntory" came from company employees saying "Torii-san" (Mr Torii). Art and religion are rife with sun imagery in Japan. Likewise, the "Suntory" name is filled with deep cultural symbolism.

Besides wine, Torii Shoten released other Western-style spirits, including a brand called Hermes in bottles that read "Old Scotch Whisky." It's unclear if the drink was actually old, Scotch or whisky. Torii, however, longed to make authentic whisky in Japan. In 1923 that became reality when ground was broken and construction started at Yamazaki. Production began a year later, but it wasn't until April 1929 that Yamazaki released the first authentic made-in-Japan whisky, Suntory Whisky, which was nicknamed Shirofuda or "white label." English covered the Scotch-style bottle, with

Left The original Konishiya headquarters hasn't changed much but the neighborhood certainly has.

Right In 1884, Konishiya established Osaka Yoshu Jozo to make and sell "whisky" among other alcoholic drinks like beer. Today, Konishi Co. Ltd focuses on making the country's best-known glue.

phrases like "Rare Old Island Whisky," a clear nod to smoky Islay whiskies. This might have been a marketing tactic to play up Western exoticism to Japanese consumers.

Priced at 4.50 yen, Shirofuda competed with slightly more expensive imported Scotch whisky brands like Johnnie Walker Red. Its release was a momentous occasion in whisky history. Torii knew it. His employees knew it. The Japanese public? Meh. Consumers not used to smoky whiskies said it "smelt burnt." Shirofuda was a failure. Yamazaki, however, followed up with another release, Suntory Akafuda (Red Label), in 1930. A red label brand might have seemed like Kotobukiya was aping Johnnie Walker Red, but along with Shirofuda (White Label), these releases show that a strong national identity was already in Japanese whisky from the start. White and red are two of the most important colors in Japan. They're found on the national flag and the country's first whiskies. Akafuda wasn't a hit either and Torii went back to his blending lab. His next creation, Suntory Kakubin, one was his greatest successes.

Released in 1937, it was originally called "Suntory Whisky 12 Year" but customers referred to it as "Kakubin" or "square bottle" and the name stuck. Not only is the whisky still on sale in Japan but it was key in resuscitating the domestic whisky business in 2007 when Suntory began a series of commercials prompting Kakubin highballs. Torii would later follow that success with iconic whiskies like Suntory Old in 1950, which was nicknamed "Daruma" because the bottle resembled a Daruma doll, based on the Buddhist monk whose legs atrophied after meditating non-stop for nine years.

Next to the Torii statue is one of his son Keizo Saji. A trained organic chemist, Saji not only followed in his father's footsteps as master blender and company president but took things a step further. Saji changed the corporate name from the vowel-heavy Kotobukiya to Suntory in 1963, believing it would play better internationally. The statue of Saji holds a 12-year-old Yamazaki single malt in his hands. "Suntory released its first single malt in 1984," Kimura says. "That was only two decades after Glenfiddich released the

first single malt in the whisky industry." In 1963, Glenfiddich released its "Straight Malt," which was the first single malt in the modern sense, even if, actually, single malts have been produced for much longer. Scotch whisky makers slowly moved to single malts during the 1970s, so Suntory didn't make that late of an entry even if it wasn't the first Japanese maker to market its whisky as such and even if the label said "Pure Malt." Yamazaki didn't have the "Single Malt" moniker until 2002–03. Technically, though, Yamazaki's maiden whisky, Shirofuda, was a single malt.

Under Saji's tenure, Suntory also released the first Hakushu single malt in 1994, following on the heels of its most acclaimed blended line, Hibiki, which launched in 1989. Saji believed that Japanese whisky shouldn't just have Japanese names but also aromas and flavors that reflected the country. Throughout his life he put tremendous emphasis on Japanese whisky's identity and wanted Suntory whiskies to have names like Yamazaki and Hibiki so they could not be mistaken for Scotch, Irish or bourbon.

Top The kanji character 響 (Hibiki) literally means "echo" or "reverberation", but it can relate to the feeling or emotion one gets when being inspired by something.
Center Tansetsu Ogino's Hibiki calligraphy captures a different emotion from Keizo Saji's Yamazaki brushwork. Ogino didn't only do Hibiki's calligraphy but also Chita's.
Below The calligraphy for 山崎 (Yamazaki) is highly stylized. As Suntory has pointed out, in Yamazaki's second kanji character 崎, the way Saji wrote 奇 looks more like 寿 (Kotobuki), making a visual reference to Suntory's former name, Kotobukiya (寿屋).

More Than Just Writing

Japanese whiskies with Japanese names and Japanese calligraphy are commonplace today but it wasn't always like that. Until the 1980s, for example, Japanese whisky labels were written in English. The thinking behind this, which is found throughout corporate Japan, was that by using international lingo it would be possible to create an international whisky that transcended identity. But Keizo Saji wanted Suntory to openly embrace the Japanese culture, so he wrote the distillery characters out in beautiful calligraphy or *shodo*. He wrote the characters for Yamazaki (山崎) that are emblazoned on Yamazaki's single malts, the distillery and the workers' uniforms, as well as the characters for Hakushu (白州).

When Saji couldn't come up with calligraphy that suited Hibiki, he asked calligrapher Tansetsu Ogino to do the honor. Today, many Japanese whisky makers feature shodo on their labels. Many are written by design firms with little connection to the distillery, but for Saji Japanese calligraphy struck at the very heart of how he saw Japanese whisky. Calligraphy can express so much through balance and brushstroke. The Japanese are judged on and judge others on their handwriting. There are correct orders for each stroke. Japanese teachers tend to be strict about how Japanese characters are written, and if anything instills an attention to detail from an early age it's the Japanese writing system. But in shodo it's not enough to nail the correct stroke order. Equally important are how the calligraphy looks aesthetically and the emotion that the calligraphy conveys.

There was a precedent. When Suntory Old was exported to the US in 1961, the bottle's label featured Shinjiro Torii's kanji calligraphy of 寿 (*kotobuki*), which means "congratulations" and "longevity." It also refers to Suntory's original name, Kotobukiya, with ya (屋), meaning "shop." Traditionally, sake bottles and shochu bottles have been covered in Japanese script but whisky bottles used to be largely English affairs. This has been one of several ways Suntory can make its whiskies look more explicitly "Japanese." Suntory, for example, uses traditional Japanese paper for its pricier single malts and blends, which is a nice touch for buyers. It has also released whiskies in evocative bottles like the Shinto *torii* gate-inspired Suntory Royal bottle or Hibiki's 24-facet bottle based on a Chinese seasonal calendar Japan imported in the 6th century called the "24 Sekki" or "24 seasonal turning points." Even though Japan shifted to the Gregorian calendar in the late 19th century, seasonal nuances are still important. But due to the country's changing climate and regional variations, the 24 Sekki feels increasingly abstract. That's not true, however, of calligraphy-covered labels.

Balance is important as is the emotion evoked through the brush strokes. "Balance" is the word that best suits Yamazaki's single malts as well as many other Japanese whiskies. It is also exactly what Suntory hoped to achieve with its first single malt. No single element of the Yamazaki single malt overwhelms or overpowers the other. There is restraint and assertion, passion and tranquility. For Suntory, all of this is best summed up in kanji calligraphy.

Left On Yamazaki's distillery tour, visitors are greeted with a beautiful Japanese garden after leaving the maturation warehouse. The waterfall and the pond, however, are man-made, with the water piped in.
Below Before visiting a Shinto shrine like Shiio Shrine, visitors perform ritual cleansing. The waterspout is in the shape of a dragon because of the creature's traditional association with water in Japan.

The Water of Yamazaki

Sitting at the base of Mt Tenno, the Yamazaki Distillery is located in the town of Shimamoto in Osaka Prefecture, bordering Kyoto Prefecture. The area known as Yamazaki is rich in history. The mountain that overlooks the distillery was strategically important to 16th-century samurai and was the site of the Battle of Yamazaki, fought here in 1582, in which the general Toyotomi Hideyoshi and his warriors avenged their fallen lord, Oda Nobunaga. Thousands were killed but the victory put Hideyoshi on his way to consolidating power across the country.

"This area was picked for several reasons," Kimura says. "One of them was its water." According to legend, 16th-century tea ceremony master Sen no Rikyu was a big fan. The local spring Rikyu no Mizu (water of the Imperial villa) is so good that Japan's Ministry of the Environment has dubbed it one of the country's one hundred best water sources.

Throughout the global whisky industry, there is currently some dispute over the importance of water in bottled whisky because of the extreme physical separations that occur during distillation. However, Suntory's chief blender Shinji Fukuyo swears by the water at Yamazaki, saying it results in a delicate and balanced spirit, and even if they use malted barley as heavily peated as you'd find in an Islay Scotch like Ardbeg, the resulting Yamazaki whisky is soft, with a gentle mouth feel and is not overpoweringly peaty.

When this location was originally chosen, it wasn't only the underground water that mattered. Past the train tracks, the Uji, Kizu and Katsura Rivers merge and flow through Osaka as the Yodo River. "Because this is where three rivers come together," says Kimura, "it means this area is often misty, which is beneficial for good whisky making." The foggiest times of the year, often early spring, the rainy season, and during the fall, are when there are wide variations in temperature and precipitation.

Endless Whisky Possibilities

Inside the distillery, the mash house is hot and there's the faint smell of baked muffins. Yamazaki hasn't malted its own barley since the early 1970s and now replies on imports. According to Shinji Fukuyo, Suntory can change the peat levels in the malt or can make the wort, the sugary liquid created after mashing malted barley, either clear or cloudy, both of which can lead to different types of whiskies. Suntory also adjusts the temperature during the whisky-making process if it wants to impart certain characteristics. Each step along the way, there is an array of options for making different whiskies.

63

Left Originally, Yamazaki's pot stills were largely uniform. Over the years, they've become incredibly diverse. Also, before Yamazaki switched to steam and direct flame, coal was shoveled in the lower lever, which is now partially covered by a walkway.

Center Two different shaped stills will result in two distinct whiskies. The pot still on the right produces a more robust spirit than the taller still on the left.

Below Brewer's beer ferments inside a Yamazaki washback that extends to the basement level below. The current Douglas fir washbacks were added during a 1988 renovation.

Behind adjacent glass doors is the fermentation room. Inside, fruity aromas—pineapples, apples and even some yogurty pears—tickle the nose. Suntory also uses different yeasts to produce different kinds of whiskies. There are eight Douglas fir Oregon pine washbacks, which extend down to the lower level below. The tops are covered, but peering in through a window, frothy foam sloshes around. "We don't have that many trees in Japan this tall that we can use for washbacks," Kimura explains. Yamazaki also has stainless steel washbacks, which are situated in another location within the distillery. Suntory believes the difference can impact the spirit, and by having both wooden and stainless steel washbacks Yamazaki is able to create an even wider array of whiskies.

The variety continues in the main still house where there is a row of twelve pot stills, six on each side. Some stills are tall and some are short. Some look like lanterns, while others look like onions, upside-down ice cream cones, or even wizard hats from *Harry Potter*. Yamazaki has another four stills, installed in 2013, in another stillroom nearby, making a grand total of sixteen. "In Japan, we don't trade whiskies," Kimura says, adding that

they have to do everything themselves. "Here's the easiest way to explain what I mean," he says, pointing to a squat still. "This makes a heavy spirit. But the tall still next to it, with the bulge in the middle, makes a clean, clear spirit."

There is even more range than just the shapes of the stills. The wash stills are direct fired by gas flame, while the spirit stills are indirect heated by steam. Originally, all the stills were coal-fired but Suntory has long phased that out.

The possibilities don't stop there, either. Most stills use condensers but a couple use worm tubs during condensation, giving the distillate further contact with copper and, thus, even more flavor. It's as though Yamazaki is a hub of several different distilleries making a dizzying number

of whiskies in-house. Then if it needs to obtain any whisky for its blends, it can tap its grain whisky distillery, Chita, or the Hakushu Distillery, which also is outfitted with a variety of different stills for making malt whisky and which makes grain whisky to boot. There's more variation in the techniques Suntory uses for maturation, which is where whisky gets most of its flavor.

The Hakushu Distillery and the Sun Grain Chita Distillery

Besides Yamazaki, the Hakushu Distillery is without a doubt Suntory's best-known whisky-making locale. It also might be Japan's most beautiful. Situated in Yamanashi Prefecture, the distillery lies within a wild bird sanctuary at the foot of Mt Kaikoma. The surrounding rivers have white sandy riverbeds from which Hakushu (白州), meaning "white sandbank," derives its name.

The Hakushu Distillery was established in 1973 to mark the 50th anniversary of the founding of Yamazaki. The idea was to make a truly modern distillery that used computers and automation to make life easier for the workers. Yamazaki itself was also modernized in the wake of Hakushu's founding. At that time, Hakushu was the biggest whisky distillery in the world.

Hakushu does share some similarities with Yamazaki, most notably the wide variety of different pot still shapes in the distillery. However, the majority of its sixteen stills are directly fired by gas. But Hakushu and Yamazaki make noticeably different whiskies, with Hakushu's forest locale coming across in the final production. Those variations mean blenders have a wider palette. "Hakushu is Hakushu and Yamazaki is Yamazaki," says Fukuyo. "There are intrinsic variations, so even if we do the same thing, the result will be different."

Key differences include a colder climate and higher elevation than Yamazaki, making for a slower aging process. Also rack-style maturation warehouses that aren't designed to hold those big sherry casks for which Yamazaki is famous. Hakushu is dominated by American white oak casks, namely 180-liter (47-gallon) barrels and 230-liter (61-gallon) hogsheads. Hakushu has an on-site cooperage, while Yamazaki's cooperage was moved to Suntory's Ohmi Aging Cellar in nearby Shiga Prefecture. When gleaming tanker trucks leave Yamazaki, they're most likely heading to Ohmi for filling and aging, or maybe Hakushu where Suntory also ages Yamazaki spirit.

Hakushu makes grain whisky, too, with production starting in 2014. Its column still churns out high-quality grain spirit that can be blended with the distillery's malt whisky for what's called a single blended whisky because it's a blend from the same place. Hakushu, however, isn't Suntory's best-known grain distillery as that honor goes to Chita. Suntory set up the Sun Grain Chita Distillery in 1972, a year before the Hakushu Distillery was established. Via towering continuous stills, Chita makes various grain whiskies, including a lighter one as well as a heavier spirit, which are then aged in various Suntory maturation warehouses, including at Yamazaki. Suntory has also been experimenting with distilling its grain spirit at different percentages of alcohol by volume in order to best find spirits that suit its needs.

Overlooking Nagoya's industrial port, Chita is certainly not as picturesque as Yamazaki or Hakushu but the whisky it makes is just as important. There are over ten different grain whiskies in Suntory's The Chita bottled release, while the distillery's whiskies continue to find their way into Hibiki's world-class blends.

Right A small Shinto shrine is located outside the main entrance to the Sun Grain Chita Distillery.

Left While the Hakushu Distillery's racked warehouses are packed with American white oak casks, the still house is, like at Yamazaki, a hodgepodge of different pot stills.

The Yamazaki of Yesteryear

On the Yamazaki Distillery tour, when you step out of the aging warehouse there's a beautiful Japanese garden. It has a small waterfall and a pond surrounded by trees that are a bright green in spring and brilliant oranges and reds in fall. "I used to live right here as a young girl," says Haruko Nakahara, now in her early eighties. "This all looked very different then. The whole distillery did, too."

Nakahara's family home sat where the man-made pond now awaits distillery tour visitors. There was no traditional Japanese garden, but there was a small field for farming. Across from that, where the current maturation warehouse is located, was another, much larger pond lined with cherry blossom trees where people would gather and admire sakura in the spring. None of that exists anymore, including the original stillhouse, save for old photos of it.

"I took this picture when I was 13," Nakahara says, holding an old photo that shows Yamazaki Distillery reflected in the pond. The composition is excellent. This was a familiar site for Nakahara because every morning when she stepped out of her house to go to school the Yamazaki Distillery was the first thing she saw. "When World War II started, we were living in central Osaka, so we moved out here to the countryside where it was safer to build a house," Nakahara says. She had just finished second grade. "I was used to living in the city and wearing shoes, but when I came here everyone was wearing *wara-zori*, straw sandals, and my feet really hurt at first."

When her father was sent off to the war, he told Haruko, his oldest daughter, to help her mother and watch her siblings. He also left her something—a camera. "My dad was into sports—skiing, hiking and even rock climbing, which was unusual for the time," Nakahara says. He started getting into photography, buying an expensive German camera as a way to remember stunning vistas. The distillery photo was how his daughter commemorated the view from their house. Even without photos, she'll never forget many things from that period. "During the war I'd watch American bombers fly over Yamazaki on their way to shell Osaka city," she says, pointing to the sky. "And since we were so close to such a large building, this distillery, I was worried they were going to bomb us, too. I thought, 'We came all the way from the city and sure picked a dangerous spot.'" The distillery wasn't shelled but much of Osaka city was flattened. "After the war, I remember seeing a truck of American soldiers pull up to the Yamazaki distillery and walk out with crate after crate of whisky."

Nakahara lived behind the distillery until she graduated from high school. As a young woman, she'd walk through the bamboo thicket behind the distillery, a small part of which is still on her family's land, to her house. Retracing those steps, distillery aromas fill the air as she climbs the hill to her family's bamboo grove, passing the local cemetery on one side and massive, yet hidden, Suntory grain silos on the other. As a girl, these smells

Taken during World War II, this photo shows the large pond that used to sit behind the Yamazaki Distillery. On the left are cherry blossom trees while on the right is a long chimney and the original distillery buildings.

Left In the right foreground is a trail that leads through Yamazaki's bamboo forest. To the left are private plots of land owned and tended by locals.
Below Autumn leaves change color in the garden behind a Yamazaki Distillery maturation warehouse. Nakahara used to call this place home, but due to extensive renovations, including new buildings and a new pond, it's completely changed from her childhood.

were the scents of her childhood. "It wasn't until I was older that I actually had whisky and I was shocked," she says. "It tasted terrible! I thought, how can something that smells so good taste so bad." Nakahara, instead, prefers sake and Shinjiro Torii's port wine blend. "As a kid, my parents would buy Akadama and they'd let us have some," she says, adding that youngsters having a glass of watered down port wine wasn't unusual in Japan in the years before World War II or in the decades that followed. "My parents thought it was okay because it was natural and made from fruit."

Nakahara walks down the main public road that cuts through the distillery. Most of the buildings aren't the originals, save for the gift shop, which used to be a Kotobukiya office. Extensive renovations over the decades have changed the distillery, but some of them haven't always been done to make whisky. The Shinto shrine gates, now at the end of the street, used to be at the beginning. At that time, people going into the distillery would pass under the Shinto gate. "I believe the reason they moved the gates was so it would be easier to get trucks down the street to the distillery," she

says. The main street, which now comprises immaculately manicured lawns and gardens, was filled with small, old houses. "People used to live on this street," she says. "Where those trees are, there used to be houses, but before the Crown Prince of Japan came in 1989 they were knocked down and Suntory trucked in big trees to plant so that the distillery would look more magnificent." In the late 1980s, the Yamazaki Distillery underwent a major multi-year overhaul to mark Suntory's 90th anniversary, but on May 16, 1989, when the Crown Prince arrived in Shimamoto, he ended up

visiting the company's R&D center and not the distillery.

After Nakahara grew up, her father later sold the land to Suntory and moved into a plot down by the railroad tracks where a former distillery manager lived. Their house was knocked down and Suntory built a Japanese garden, complete with a small pond. Nakahara still calls Shimamoto home, and recently Suntory has been pumping whisky-making water from the plot right next to hers. "I guess wherever I live," Nakahara says, "I won't be able to escape Suntory." At least not near Yamazaki, that is.

Where Suntory Whisky Sleeps

Over 10,000 whisky-filled casks quietly sleep at Yamazaki. The distillery uses five different cask sizes but is dominated by 480-liter (127-gallon) puncheons made from American white oak. There is also a large number of 480-liter sherry casks, but Suntory will not give an exact number. "You can tell the sherry casks by looking for the ones imprinted with KTB," Kimura says, pointing. "It refers to Kotobukiya. The sherry maker in Spain who crafted these casks does that so it knows which ones are ours." Originally, when the distillery was founded, Yamazaki exclusively used sherry casks made from European oak, which are known for their fragrant dark fruit and spicy flavors. During World War II, however, the distillery had trouble procuring them and turned to *mizunara* or Japanese oak (for more on mizunara, see pages 37–38). Today, mizunara casks are instrumental in Yamazaki's maturation process. They are, however, also preciously rare. We can only make 100–150 mizunara casks each year,"

Kimura says. To put that into context, Suntory has over one million casks in its warehouses. Mizunara is only a very tiny, yet very special, sliver in that number. There isn't that much mizunara suitable for cask making for Suntory to produce more. At Yamazaki's maturation warehouse, mizunara casks can be picked out in one of two ways. On the cask's head there is either an imprinted "J" or a box around the abbreviation "No." Often there are both.

Suntory's blenders have also used maturation techniques that are unique to Japan. Abroad, whiskies are sometimes "finished" in wine casks at the end of maturation to add flavors and aromas, a process Suntory does, too, but since the Yamazaki Distillery also makes *umeshu* (plum wine), blenders have also experimented with moving whiskies into umeshu casks for a short period in a home-grown style of finishing. Suntory also ages whiskies in *sugi* or Japanese cedar, a unique whisky maturation method. There is a tradition of doing this as some sake is given a quick finish in sugi Japanese-style

This Yamazaki warehouse is filled with large 480-liter (127-gallon) casks, most famously mizunara and sherry butts. Whisky distilled at Yamazaki is put in casks with white heads. Spirit from the Sun Grain Chita Distillery is put in casks with black heads, while in Hakushu's racked warehouses, bourbon barrels rule, but sherry and virgin American white oak casks are also used.

casks—long enough to give it a distinct aroma but not too long to color or overpower the sake. Japanese cedar has a sharp scent, and according to chief blender Shinji Fukuyo, Suntory only uses a "tiny bit" in its Torys blends. "It works well at lifting up the top note and also bringing out other aromas," Fukuyo says. "When people raise their glass for a *kanpai* in Japan, they often make highballs with carbonated water and ice cubes. Japanese cedar works best for that kind of whisky." Under the previous chief blender, Seiichi Koshimizu, Suntory released a blend called "Za" in 2000, designed to go with Japanese food and made with whisky matured in Japanese cedar. According to Suntory, only "one part" of these

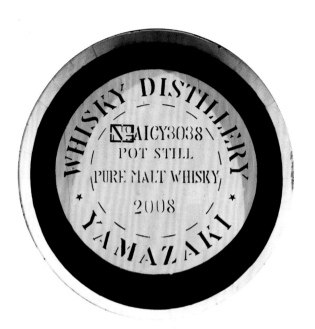

casks—namely, the heads or lids—were made with indigenous cedar. The sugi-aged whisky hasn't been released as a special single malt, though Fukuyo says that would be interesting.

Since the spirit Yamazaki distills is delicate and soft, it can be influenced greatly by the cask during maturation. "Compared to Scotch whisky, Japanese whisky is even more influenced by the cask," says Fukuyo. "The temperature in Japan is perfect for this. If you go to hotter climates, the maturation might be too fast." Because whisky matures much more quickly in Japan, Suntory must monitor its casks closely. "As blenders we must be careful with any whisky over 15 years old because the cask influence can be too strong," says Fukuyo. "Thus, we would do things like move the whisky to an older cask or perhaps store it in a cooler part of the maturation warehouse. More so than in Scotland, if we don't properly handle the maturation, our older whisky won't age well."

Yamazaki is a beautiful spot in which to age whisky but not all of

it is matured at the famed distillery. Yamazaki spirit is also aged off-site, hauled some four plus hours away to its forest-covered sister distillery Hakushu. Most goes an hour away to the Ohmi Aging Cellar in Shiga Prefecture, which is slightly cooler in the winter than the Yamazaki Distillery as it gets more snow, but is almost as hot in summer. The massive Ohmi Aging Cellar maturation complex is not open to

the public. A few photos exist from the 1990s, showing roads leading to individually numbered warehouses painted with the English words "Cellar." To meet high demand, in 2014 Suntory built a 6,000-sq meter (650,000-sq ft) maturation warehouse there that's able to hold another 130,000 casks, and in 2017 built another one of the same size to age Yamazaki and Hakushu whiskies. Ohmi also has a cooperage, which is larger than the one at Hakushu, which makes and refurbishes casks for Yamazaki.

The Secrets Of Suntory's Signature Blending Process

"Before I became a blender I never really thought deeply about what the job involved," says Suntory Whisky's chief blender Shinji Fukuyo. The common notion is that the gig entails wearing a white lab coat while nosing and tasting hundreds of different whiskies. Blenders do that, but there's much more to it.

Decked out in a Yamazaki uniform, Fukuyo sits in a room overlooking a bamboo forest and a small Japanese garden. Behind him is a fully stocked bar lined with Yamazaki, Hakushu and Hibiki. When he joined Suntory in 1984, he didn't start here at Yamazaki but at the Hakushu Distillery in Yamanashi Prefecture. "While there, blenders would come to check the whisky we were distilling and aging, and I remember realizing that there were people doing this as a job." Internally at Suntory, there were—and still are—tests to see which employees have good noses. "The tests ask you to do things like pick out which whisky smells different or to line up seven whiskies with similar aromas in increasing intensity," says Fukuyo. "I always did well and I threw myself into learning more."

Fukuyo's mentor was on the blending team at Yamazaki, and when there was an opening he was brought on board, in 1992. "When I first joined, my time training was spent learning about the various aromas and flavors," he says. After that, he began studying more about blending and blending techniques. "Being able to pick out different smells is very different from being able to create different aromas," he says. When the blenders get to work, Fukuyo says, the process requires more time. "You have to think about the shape of the whisky from top to bottom," he adds—the whisky's top note, the mouth feel, the finish and how it tastes on the rocks or as a cocktail.

At Suntory, the blenders have basic guidelines about what they won't eat. For breakfast they don't have traditional Japanese meals with grilled fish because the oil stays on the palette throughout the day. At dinner they don't eat garlic because it lingers. "Among blenders here, sometimes we can tell when someone on the team had garlic and we'll call them out, and they'll deny it even though we can still smell it. Then they'll slowly realize that, yes, the salad dressing from last night had garlic in it."

Every day for lunch, Fukuyo eats *soba* (buckwheat noodles) with *tempura*, following in the footsteps of Suntory's previous chief blender, Seiichi Koshimizu, who ate *udon* noodles with *tempura*. Fukuyo says he does so for several reasons. One, he doesn't have to think about what he's going to have for lunch, and since the meal is light he can get back to work right after he eats. Another reason is because eating the same thing makes his palette more sensitive to changes in flavor—at least, in the soba broth. "When you eat the same thing every day, you notice how the flavor changes from day to day," he says. That, in turn, makes him more responsive to those who regularly drink Suntory's whiskies and thus might be aware of subtle changes. "I'm always concerned about the opinions of these customers, because if there is the slightest variation they let us know right away," he says. "For me, eating the same food every day is similar, because you become aware of subtle differences and do your best to keep the whisky's signature flavor and aroma from changing." Managing available whisky stock to keep signature single malts and blends is one of the chief blender's unsung duties.

"We've done things that are new and not traditionally done in Scotland," says Shinji Fukuyo, who became Suntory's fourth chief blender in 2009. "I want to continue to break new boundaries in whisky."

putting out as much as we can but the demand from outside the country is larger than we foresaw a decade ago." For the Yamazaki 12 year old, managing the whisky means ensuring there is enough whisky to go into the single malt. "In the Yamazaki 12 year old, we use whiskies that are 12 years old and older," Fukuyo says. "If we don't ensure we have enough of these whiskies to make the 12-year-old single malt, then we could have a year in which we couldn't release any bottles of it." So, what's Suntory's solution? Make a wide variety of whiskies. "For example, if the 12 year old Yamazaki is only a blend of three whiskies, then that means if one of them changes in flavor or is in short supply then it's impossible to make that whisky," Fukuyo says. "That's why, for us it's important to make over 10 different types of whisky to use in this single malt to ensure stability." For Suntory, making a wide variety of whiskies is paramount. "By blending them, we can keep the single malt's signature flavor and aromas". That might be Suntory's biggest secret of all.

Above "My job isn't only to ensure quality," says Fukuyo, "but to ensure that we have enough whisky."

Right The Hibiki blends contain malt and grain whiskies from Suntory's Yamazaki, Hakushu and Chita distilleries.

"When we are looking at a large number of whiskies for, let's say, the Yamazaki 12 year old," he says, pointing to a row of Yamazaki single malts, "we'll line up 200 or 300 samples of sherried whisky that we are thinking of using for this single malt." This process, as daunting as it might seem, isn't the most difficult part of the blender's job. "It's actually easier to go through and pick out the differences between similar whiskies," says Fukuyo. "Basically, finding one that stands out is like looking at a field of yellow flowers and spotting the rogue white ones." If, these days making old whiskies is hard enough, then making a new whisky is when things get difficult. In the past few years in Japan, because of the enormous popularity of Yamazaki's whiskies, it's become difficult to find single malts with age statements. Even the 12 year old, a standard release, can be hard to come by even in Japan. "We're

An Ideal Place to Make Whisky

"This is a sherry cask Yamazaki single malt," Toshikazu Kimura says, raising his glass and putting it to his nose. "The 2013 release was called the best whisky in the world." This whisky has a delightful nose with raisins, dark chocolate and toffee. Taking a sip, it's soft and smooth. Kimura puts down the glass of sherry cask Yamazaki and takes the glass next to it. "This was aged in our mizunara casks," he says. "The aroma rises quickly through the nose." His tasting notes are sandalwood, incense and old kimono. You could add Japanese fans and paper sliding doors to that list. "It's a gentle yet complex scent," he adds. Often Western whisky writers—and even Suntory itself—say whisky aged in mizunara has "Oriental aromas."

The word "Oriental" in Japan, seen in the likes of the ritzy Oriental Hotel, is perceived as fancy and regal. In English, the word isn't only loaded but it doesn't make much distinction between Japan and its neighboring Asian countries. A better description would be "Japanese." It is strong, subtle and holds its own in blends, just as Japaneseness has continued to shine throughout the centuries despite the importation of Chinese and Western culture. Few whiskies strike at the heart of the Japanese character like mizunara-aged ones.

"If you don't mature whisky in mizunara for a long time, you don't get these aromas," Kimura says. "If you blend mizunara-aged whisky, these aromas expand." It's a strong, sturdy whisky with a stronger sense of character than you'd think. Both the sherried and the mizunara-aged whiskies give the distillery much of its character.

But its character isn't only dependent on the whisky that is distilled. It's also the surroundings. It's Yamazaki itself—those tiny cramped streets, the foggy mornings, the bamboo forests and the festivals at Shiio Shrine. Walking outside that late summer afternoon, laughing children are now out of school and lugging their backpacks down the street, through the distillery and up to their homes. They pass the reception booth, greet workers with chipper hellos and continue on their way.

The sun is cooling off, the air feels fresh and there's a rustle of wind. The mountain behind the distillery is a lush green. This truly is an ideal place to make whisky.

TASTING NOTES FOR 29 SUNTORY WHISKIES

By Yuji Kawasaki

Suntory makes a range of whiskies from budget-priced supermarket stuff to premium single malts and blends. It's famous for its ability to deftly use different casks in maturation to make truly wonderful whiskies. The Yamazaki single malts are slightly floral but round and heavy, leaving a strong impression. The Hakushu single malts are fresh and leafy, reminiscent of late spring and early summer. The Hibiki blends are not only soft and sweet but unbelievably layered, nuanced and deep. If anything best represents Japanese whisky, it's the elegant Hibiki blends.

The Chita 61/100

Hailing from Suntory's Sun Grain Chita Distillery in Nagoya Port, this isn't a single malt distilled in pot stills but a grain whisky made in towering continuous stills. The Chita smells of charred cereals and brownies. There's some high-pitched sweetness, but in the middle of the boutique things get pungent. That sweetness comes though faintly in the flavor, like freshly made cornflakes. However, the wheels come off and whole thing quickly falls apart. File this one under "for mixers."

The Hakushu Single Malt Whisky Sherry Cask Bottled In 2012 82/100

Ah, the annual sherry casks. Here we have the 2012 edition for the Hakushu Distillery. Besides the obvious sherry aromas, wood that's reminiscent of an old desk dominates. Sharp, acidic notes stand out, but thankfully so does sweet chocolate. Perhaps, a sufficient starter to those new to the world of sherried Japanese whiskies. Perhaps.

The Hakushu Single Malt Whisky (No Age Statement) 56/100

In the bouquet, the amount of alcohol sticks out like a thorn. (Could that sharpness be that this whisky is aimed at highballs?) Once you get past the alcohol, discover camomile and the slight scent of an open-air fire in a deep wood. Taking a sip, watery strawberries appear on arrival. But that's about it. There are only faint berry-type flavors and not much complexity, supporting the case that this is intended for cocktails.

The Hakushu Single Malt 12 Years Old 82/100

The smell of a forest on a clear day during the rainy season. The tree's vitality is in full force, and on palette the flavors are sweet and unripe. But, like a sudden downpour, those leafy notes are washed away for a long, relaxing woody finish.

The Hakushu Single Malt Whisky 18 Years Old 88/100

Imagine a forest. If a short, eloquent piece of music were to be played on a piano and with a flute you'd want gentle light, fresh foliage filling the air and some raspberries in the grass. That's this Hakushu single malt. It

The Chita

Hakushu Single Malt Whisky 18 Years Old

Hakushu Single Malt Whisky 25 Years Old

Hibiki 17 Years Old

Hibiki 21 Years Old

grows wild but it's been cultured. The arrival is clear and graceful, and you can hear the babbling of a brook. Gathered dried wood is laid out on the ground and the smell of it being lit fills the air. Here's a single malt to be experienced and enjoyed.

The Hakushu Single Malt Whisky 25 Years Old 89/100

The nose is sweet and crisp. You are again transported to a forest, or a moss-covered Shinto shrine, and there's the rich smell of earth after a rain. It's leisurely, like taking a stroll. Other aromas: Lemons, flowers, and smoke. Tasting this 25-year-old Hakushu is a rich experience underscored by chocolate and figs. Yet, even the palette still transports you back to that forest grove, with wet leaves and unripe fruit on the trees for a brief moment of tranquil happiness.

Hibiki Deep Harmony 97/100

Released in June 2013, Hibiki Deep Harmony was exclusive to Japanese bars but bottles have popped up on online shops and auction sites. Deep Harmony features malt whiskies

matured in red wine casks and grain whisky aged in sherry casks. The result is a beautiful blend. There are the dark fruits you'd expect but also soft and gentle aromas. Every single scent has its unique component, making Deep Harmony liquid poetry. It's Japanese sliding doors, a tatami room with a flower vase in an alcove and a bird fluttering from a branch. In a whisky, it's rare to see such beauty as this.

Hibiki Japanese Harmony 86/100

Nosing the glass, the first note smells like fresh ink from a fountain pen, followed by honeyed wood aromas from the cask. The delivery is astonishingly soft, covering the mouth in what feels like flowing silk. For such a humble boutique, the texture of this whisky is a gourmet meal! Even though this whisky offers an uncommon experience, it does lack complexity.

Hibiki 12 Years Old 76/100

Hibiki is synonymous with pre-eminent blended Japanese whisky. In 2009, Suntory launched this 12 year version. It's grassy and smells of burnt fields. There's also a cherry note and

the scent of sakura cascading over a brook. Taste wise, there's a gentle spiciness. Behind that, though, there's the hard candy sold at Japanese festivals as well as the sweet sourness of unripe persimmons. Not the best Hibiki has to offer.

Hibiki 17 Years Old 93/100

Gently swirl the glass and you're overcome with springtime scents. You can see a beautiful field of flowers. Bees buzzing. Perfect weather. You want to find a hammock for an afternoon nap. That's the depth of the aroma. It's not just on the nose but also in the taste. Even though this is a crafted whisky, it's as natural and relaxed as they come without appearing to try hard.

Hibiki 21 Years Old 85/100

Here we go, another Hibiki. Another prime representation of Japanese blended whisky. Saying that this is an example of the soul of Japan really makes the image of Japanese people far too serious. However, this whisky is certainly delicious.

As for the bouquet, there's eggplant, corn and an organic solvent smell.

Hibiki 30 Years Old

Suntory Blended Whisky Houga

Suntory Royal

Behind that, there's the smell of oak and fresh rain, refreshing wild grass in summer and earthy soil. This Hibiki just dissolves in the mouth like toffee. Even though it's thick and heavy, the whisky is balanced and there's no astringency. Each part of this whisky reveals itself bit by bit, with dignity. Metallic flavors, red clay, clean water and grass. The finish is long and seems to keep going. A very floral and very Japanese whisky.

Hibiki 30 Years Old 91/100
The nose is wrapped in sweetness— sugary pineapple, strawberries and bananas. Taking a sip, it's delicious, caramelized honey from top to bottom, which is certainly a Hibiki signature for a long finish. Yet, in this 30 year there is a nostalgia that simply doesn't exist in other Hibiki expressions, like the warmth of a good orchestral recording playing on large wooden speakers. This blend is truly a work of art.

Suntory Blended Whisky Houga 86/100
A blend of older Suntory whiskies, this is limited to only 500 bottles.

"Hou" (鳳) refers to "Houou" (鳳凰) or "phoenix," the mythical bird that appears when a ruler is right and just. (Note that the phoenix of the Eastern tradition is different from the fiery bird of the West.) "Ga" (雅) means "elegance." This whisky is certainly that! There's the scent of a fountain pen and freshly written ink, followed by honeyed wood. The arrive is astonishingly soft, flowing into the mouth like silk, bringing a regal texture and refined flavors that are akin to a worn and well-accustomed amber-colored pipe. Houga offers a unique experience but one without nuance.

Suntory Kakubin Whisky 56/100
Roasted barley aromas but wrapped in a sweetness that's accompanied by corn, oak and peppermint. The arrival is smooth, showing the sweetness and the subtleness of the casks. But that sensation quickly vanishes and the grain asserts itself right on through the finish. Granted, this is a well-blended whisky. The sweetness and minty notes are refreshing, but Kakubin posseses a bitterness that asserts there are more delicious flavors than just sweet.

Currently, this is the biggest selling whisky in Japan. It's approachable, friendly and ideal for those who might not enjoy Suntory's more serious blends and single malts. Kakubin is a warm welcome to the world of Japan whisky. Much better stuff lies ahead.

Suntory Single Grain Whisky Chita Distillery 68/100
A limited release of Suntory's Chita grain whisky. Sweet flower nectar notes, but this also seems rather rugged. Clean water on wood appears on arrival. Those elements still feel separated and don't quite come together. There's no personality, really, leaving you wondering when any uniqueness is going to show up.

Suntory Red 74/100
Well-rounded and floral but thorny. You get cinnamon, lemon and sesame. The savory whisky aromas are enjoyable momentarily but soon vanish. Suntory Red would probably be good with creamy food. It's not a complicated blend but is definitely assertive.

Yamazaki (No Age Statement)

Yamazaki Single Malt 12 Years Old

Yamazaki Single Malt 18 Years Old

Suntory Za Japanese Bler

Suntory Royal **76/100**

Lush honey. Hypnotic sherry. For better or worse the aromas have no other nuances. Taking a sip, Royal seems to melt in the mouth within seconds, like toffee. The body is delicate and not too thick but not too fine. An uncomplicated whisky with dreams of luxury.

Suntory White **63/100**

The contemporary heir of Shirofuda, Yamazaki's first whisky, is a lower-priced (and less smoky) version of the original release. On the nose you're reminded of white flowers. However, that quickly turns to alcohol. Suntory White isn't a whisky that is pretending to be more than it isn't—much like those tiny restaurants under elevated track trains in Tokyo and Osaka. You stumble in at 3 am, you just want something hot and bam, there you go. Ditto for Suntory White. Surprisingly, as noticeable as the alcohol is, White barely suits the subtle flavors of the Japanese palette.

Suntory Za **68/100**

The most noteworthy thing about this blend is the way it's made. Suntory aged a portion of the Za spirit in oak barrels with Japanese cedar heads (lids). Za launched it in 2000, but even though it's no longer in production old bottles can sometimes be found in Japanese liquor stores. The cedar, however, isn't readily apparent—or at all. There's the smell of a burnt match. *Kuromitsu* (dark sugar syrup) candy and a red bean jelly Japanese dessert that you'd eat with a toothpick.

Suntory Zen **80/100**

Suntory distilled this malt spirit via a continous still and filtered it through bamboo charcoal. That's interesting. Production ended in 2010 but bottles still turn up at liquor stores in Japan. A sweet oak scent. Pastoral wheat and the smell of late autumn. Slight bitterness.

Torys Extra **52/100**

Fragrantly soft barley notes and the sweetness of wort are what hit you first. But there are also flowery nectar, banana, pineapple and fig aromas.

Those notes, along with the taste of alcohol, are only strengthened on arrival. Fruity and clear, this seems like a whisky that wouldn't be worth writing home about but has more teeth than you'd expect.

The Yamazaki Single Malt Whisky Heavily Peated Bottled in 2013 **56/100**

The label says "Heavily Peated" but this whisky smells of fruit, such as berries. It is peaty but the peat smells fragrant to the point of fruity. Taking a sip, rather gentle cask notes are followed up by stimulation of alcohol. Other flavors? Peat and peppery spices. It's all rather calm and well rounded.

But the label says "Heavily peated"! For people who like Yamazaki single malts, this whisky is perhaps most suitable as an educational introduction to the world of peated whiskies. It's wonderful that Suntory makes limited edition bottlings like this. However, beyond that there really isn't much appeal here. The peat doesn't come across as heavy. This should be called "Yamazaki Somewhat Peated."

Suntory Zen Pure Malt Whisky

The Yamazaki Single Malt Whisky Mizunara Bottled in 2012 88/100

The aromas are refreshing, youthfully vibrant. There are some slight charred notes, and the mizunara cask aroma conveys gentle, yet fragrant *umami*. The nose is reminiscent of a newly constructed wooden Japanese house. The delivery is also refreshing, with good, soft mouthfeel. A bitterness slightly brings out the savory flavors. The finish doesn't coat the entire mouth but, interestingly, only coats the tongue. It's a sensation that you don't experience with whiskies aged in a typical cask. The result is a vibrant, weighty whisky that's certainly unique.

The Yamazaki Single Malt Plum Liqueur Cask Finish 87/100

Limited to only 3,000 bottles, this 12-year-old single malt was released in 2008. It's made from mizunara-aged and European oak-aged whiskies that were finished in *umeshu* (plum liqueur) casks for another two years.

It's like the nose is covered with a beautiful yellow or red veil. Sweet and gentle aromas, and you can imagine how the essence of the plum liqueur seeped in bit by bit. Tightly packed aromas expand gently. The lovely acidic notes are characteristic of umeshu. Charred cask and matured cherries. Enchanting.

The Yamazaki Single Malt Whisky (No Age Statement) 74/100

The initial boutique is honey. However, the scent of wooden boards gets in the way. Taking a sip, there's sweetness, but it's like the inside of your mouth is then stabbed with splinters. The finish is hot and like a wave that just keeps going and going, destroying any semblance of balance and seeming to possess a runner's strong will. It won't quit. This isn't a harmonious whisky, but the way it asserts itself is worthy of mention.

The Yamazaki Single Malt Whisky 12 Years Old 83/100

This whisky had a successful series of commercials during the 1990s featuring images of red maple leaves, pink cherry blossoms and bamboo thickets. The ads were important in showing Japanese whisky embracing own native sensibilities instead of looking to the West as it had done for so many years. So, how is this classic Japanese single malt? There are charred and honeyed oak notes on the nose, the smell of a grassy field after rain and some gentle smoke. It's smooth, with lovely texture that just appears to hang in the mouth, followed up with a wonderfully spicy finish.

The Yamazaki Single Malt Whisky 18 Years Old 85/100

Lots of lovely fresh tree and floral notes. It's like dipping your nose in a Japanese forest in June, filled with new, bright green leaves and wildflowers. In the distance, there's some smoke—kindling, to be exact. Taking a sip, all those aromas expand and you can really taste the floral notes as well as the smoke.

The Yamazaki Single Malt Whisky 25 Years Old 89/100

This is one of Suntory's super premium offerings, with bottles getting snapped up as soon as they appear, only to resurface online where they easily command prices in the thousands. Sherried whiskies dominate, but first impressions are the aromas of a dense forest. Fire crackles and the smell of logs burning in a brick stove fill the air. Cool darkness descends and the forest returns, but rather noisily. Warming spices—like in a salty soup—for a soporific finish.

The Yamazaki 1999 The Owner's Cask Mampei Hotel 98/100

This single cask Yamazaki was distilled in 1999 and bottled in 2015 for the Mampei Hotel in Karuizawa. It's served at the hotel but there are a few bottles floating around online for purchase.

Truly wonderful scents rise right out of the glass. There's a fullness, with a tinge of light elegance that extends through the aromas. That gives way to delightfully crisp and heavier spice notes. Tastewise, it's as though the best notes have been wrung out of muscat grapes. You can't find muscat grape flavors this good in even the most superior Darjeeling teas! The finish, though, isn't neat and tidy but hot. There is one word for this Yamazaki and that is sublime.

EIGASHIMA SHUZO
WHITE OAK WHISKY DISTILLERY

The sun beats down on the rocky pier, which juts out into the Inland Sea. A shirtless man sits on the rocks fishing. There are the sounds of gently lapping waves and ship motors droning in the distance, and only a short walk away is the White Oak Whisky Distillery.

"Personally, I can't taste sea salt in our whiskies," says Mikio Hiraishi, president of Eigashima Shuzo, the company that owns the distillery. "But it's no mystery when people say they can."

Located in Akashi, 45 minutes or so away from Kobe, the distillery is across the street from Eigashima Shuzo's main gig, sake brewing. Distinctive Japanese roofs and wooden walls contrast with European-style yellow window

shutters, potted plants hanging from the sills and a rooster weather vein perched on the pagoda of the whisky distillery. Inside, master sake brewers are spending their summer making fine, lightly peated whiskies.

Whisky Made by Sake Brewers

Traditionally, this area is famous for sake production. Hiraishi's great-grandfather founded Eigashima Shuzo in 1888 after five sake breweries merged into a single entity. Sake was, and still is, Eigashima Shuzo's main meal ticket, but in 1919 it decided to expand and got a whole host of liquor licenses, including the right to make wine, brandy and whisky. "At that time, proper whisky wasn't made here," Hiraishi says. "I'm not

really sure, but I think we just blended imported Scotch whisky and aged it."

Eigashima Shuzo sold small amounts of whisky before and during World War II, but not figures of much merit and nothing like Suntory or Nikka. Among foreign drinks, wine was far more important. In 1921, it launched Shirodama or "White Ball" white wine, promoting it with a motor car, a novelty at that time, to portray Eigashima Shuzo as a regal and modern company. Initially, Shirodama was a hard sell

Left Eigashima Shuzo's first pot stills from circa 1964.
Below right The copper wash in the foreground holds 4,500 liters (1,200 gallons) while the spirit still in the background holds 3,000 liters (793 gallons). The bottom of the stills are from the now-shuttered Silver Whisky Distillery in Nara, while the tops were refurbished by Miyake Industries.
Below left The White Oak Distillery is across the street from Eigashima Shuzo's sake brewery.

because then most Japanese thought wine was red, no doubt thanks in part to the success of Akadama Port Wine (see pages 59–60).

As whisky became more and more popular after World War II, Eigashima Shuzo began distilling it in the mid-1960s. Since sake is traditionally made only in winter, whisky became a way for Eigashima Shuzo, and other sake brewers as well, to expand their portfolio. Since sake does not have a long shelf life and because production is seasonal, whisky making could supplement business.

"These are the first stills," Hiraishi says, pointing to a pair sitting outside in a small atrium. "They were only 1,000-liter [264-gallon] stills, because we didn't make or sell much whisky." The 1980s brought the *ji-uisukii* or "local whisky" boom, with the bottle keep system encouraging customers to buy their own bottles at snack bars across Japan. Sales were brisk enough to encourage Eigashima Shuzo to build a new distillery in 1984 with refurbished stills.

Eigashima Shuzo doesn't make whisky all year round but only distills from April to July. The others months are largely dedicated to making sake as well as wine. Typically, Japanese distilleries shut down for June and July for maintenance because summer is just too damn hot, but the White Oak Distillery keeps distilling. "We used to make whisky year round," Hiraishi says. "We had dedicated distillers working here who only made whisky." Then, at around the turn of the century, with the whisky business at record lows in Japan, the White Oak Distillery began seasonal distilling. During the fall and winter, the craftsmen work as brewers, making sake, and during the spring and summer they work as distillers, making whisky.

"In Japan, the tradition has been that during the colder months villagers would come to a sake brewery to work. Once the sake was made and the weather warmed up in the spring, they'd return to their fields to work through summer and the fall harvest," says Hirashi. "These days, those kinds of people don't really exist anymore."

However, the pace of life at Eigashima Shuzo continues to reflect those seasonal rhythms, with liquor production changing with the weather. "I do think that the fact we distill in the summer does affect the whisky," says Hirashi. It might make fermentation easier, but to what effect he doesn't know. "Maybe the biggest impact is that making whisky is harder," he says with a chuckle. "It gets so darn hot in here."

An electric fan spins in front of the lauter tun. It's not to cool the distillery equipment but the distillers. "It's unbelievably hot in July," says Hiroki Hasegawa, who's been at Eigashima Shuzo for over 30 years. New wall fans were recently installed.

"The seasonal changes keep our job fun," Hasegawa says. "It's also fun because what we make people seem to enjoy." He checks the temperature of the mash and pencils in numbers on a chart. There doesn't seem to be a computer in sight. Here things are done the old fashioned way. By hand.

Now that whisky is once again popular in Japan, Hiraishi says he'd like to make more. "But," he adds with a smile, "if we brought in people who

only made whisky, when spring and summer rolls around our sake brewers would have nothing to do." Depending on the demand for whisky and sake, Eigashima Shuzo has the flexibility to shorten or lengthen the production periods for each.

Sake Techniques to Make Whisky

"Out of all the different alcoholic drinks we make, I personally think sake is the most difficult," says Hirashi, adding that it's incredibly tricky to find the delicate balance while the mash is undergoing glucose conversion at the same time that fermentation is taking place.

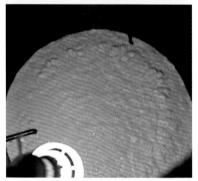

Far right top Distillery worker Hiroki Hasegawa checks the mash tun. White Oak uses imported malted barley lightly peated at 10 ppm.
Far right center A yeast starter known in Japanese as shubo is made in dedicated tanks.
Far right Shubo is highly concentrated and ensures greater control during fermentation. When making shubo, White Oak uses mass-produced distiller's yeast or, starting in 2017, ale yeast.
Right Unaged distillate or "new-make" spirit is clear. It changes color during maturation in wood casks.

Left Master whisky distiller Yuji Nakamura checks to see when to "make the cut." The best part of the distillation, known as the heart, is collected in a holding tank below, called the spirit receiver.
Below New distillate running off the still.

Above While water boils at 100 °C (212 °F), alcohol's boiling point is lower, 78 °C (172 °F). Pictured is the tail end of a distillation run.
Above center New distillate flows through the spirit safe. The master distiller checks the temperature and the spirit to know which parts will be cut for maturation and which parts will be recycled back for further distillation.
Above right Interestingly, the Eigashima Shuzo spirit safe is so low to the ground that workers must crouch over to check it.

Whisky making, Hirashi explains, is far more straightforward and ordered. It's step by step, unlike sake brewing, when at times everything can seem to be happening at once. "You don't have as much to worry about when making whisky," Hirashi says, adding, "If you know how to make sake, then you have a good idea of how whisky is made." And if you're a sake brewer, then your tool kit is bound to be bigger.

"Your typical whisky maker uses a brewer's yeast or buys an industrial distiller's yeast," says Hirashi. "But with the yeast we then create what's called *shubo* in Japanese, which is a mash starter that's a normal part of the sake-making process, so this one part of our whisky process is similar." Shubo (酒母) literally means "alcohol" and "mother," and in sake production it

directly impacts the finished flavor. When making whisky, the grist is steeped in hot water to turn the complex starches into simple sugars, creating mash. This is then filtered into the sugary liquid known as wort, which is key for fermenting alcohol. Instead of putting the wort directly into the large washbacks and then plopping in the yeast, like Scottish distillers typically do, sugary wort is added into a smaller separate container with a little bit of yeast for fermentation. Growth is cultured and more is created. The result is a pure, highly concentrated yeast starter.

It's time-consuming and difficult, but by using a concentrated shubo yeast starter, White Oak helps prevent any off flavors during fermentation, which can easily occur in humid Japan. Sake and whisky are different drinks. They're made in different ways. Yuji Nakamura is the master whisky distiller, but that is only his part-time job at Eigashima Shuzo, because he's also a *toji* or master sake brewer. "Since this is originally a sake brewery," he says, "it's only natural we'd use shubo during whisky fermentation." This could also be why Nikka, founded by the son of a sake brewer, also makes shubo for fermentation.

Japan's Distilling Tradition

Nakamura walks over to the spirit safe, opens it up and checks the temperature. Distilled spirit pours out, but he's looking for the optimal part of the distilled run, called the heart, which is filled with the desired flavor compounds and characteristics.

The master sake brewer checks the temperature again and makes the cut, changing the flow of the distilled spirit from the heads to the heart, or the middle cut, which is collected in the spirit receiver below. Once he finishes making the cut, the flow of the whisky will switch back over and the heads and the tails of the distillation will be cycled back into the still and distilled once again. White Oak is aiming for a distilled spirit that is 67 alcohol by volume, which it then cuts with water, bringing down the alcohol percentage before the spirit is put in casks for aging. "You know, Japan has its own distilling tradition," he says, closing the spirit safe's lid. "The tradition was to distill the spirit only one time. However, the tradition in Europe is to distill two or three times and great emphasis is put on aging in casks."

The Japanese distilling tradition he's referring to is *shochu*, which Nakamura

Above The White Oak Whisky Distillery's warehouses are dominated by bourbon barrels but there are also a number of sherry casks as well as ex-shochu ones. Wine casks from Eigashima Shuzo's winery are also used for "finishing" whiskies.

Below Whisky straight from the cask. The beautiful amber color is the result of maturation.

Below right While Eigashima Shuzo got its first whisky distilling license in 1919, the current distillery building was built in 1984.

adds can be aged in stainless steel tanks or, as it's traditionally been done, in clay pots. Shochu can be, and indeed is, also aged in casks for up to three years, or even longer, but the shochu distillers aim to retain much of the original flavor of the grain, unlike whisky distillers who layer a wide array of aromas and flavors on their spirit. In the past, Eigashima Shuzo regularly produced shochu but in recent years has focused more on whisky (for more on shochu, see pages 15–16).

The White Oak Warehouses

Two aging ivy covered warehouses sit side by side, while a third is located elsewhere on the distillery grounds. Inside one it's breezy but hot. Windows are cracked open and grated screens keep bugs out. The smell filling the warehouse is soft and mellow. There's honey and vanilla with lingering raisins. Ex-bourbon barrels dominate, but there are also some sherry butts and even shochu casks. "This is a shochu cask made by independent cooper Ariake Barrel," Hiraishi says, pointing. The cask is beautifully made, with the company's logo branded into the wood. "Shochu doesn't leave much flavor in the cask because it's not such a strong smelling spirit compared to, say, bourbon," Hiraishi says. "If you char a shochu cask, it's close to a new one."

On a nearby cask, "2013" is scrawled in pink chalk. "We don't have much old

whisky," Hiraishi says, as the distillery is selling through whatever it makes. Several rows of casks line up on planks on the concrete floor. In the back of the warehouse are half-filled racks.

White Oak's no-age statement single malt is at least three years old, but it gets sweltering at the distillery and doesn't taste as young as it is. "You don't need to mature it so long here because it's so hot," Hiraishi says, blotting his brow with a handkerchief. "We can mature whisky probably several times faster than in Scotland."

Self-reliant Japanese Whisky

Yet, even with the nods to Scotland, the use of imported Scottish barley and Scottish grain whisky for its budget-priced blends, the White Oak Distillery isn't simply rehashing Scotch whisky in a seaside Japanese town. "It's not like we've gone to Scotland to learn whisky production," says Hirashi, opening the door to go back outside. "We've had to figure out things for ourselves."

Unlike in Scotland, though, in Japan there isn't only a lack of trading whisky but there isn't much trading of information either. "In Japan, huge whisky makers dominate, so there's not much opportunity to develop a working relationship with them or learn from them," says Hirashi. "Recently, we have been talking whisky making with the smaller makers, like Mars and Chichibu, which is helpful." In the past, he adds, that didn't really happen, leaving the distillery to rely on its own experience in brewing sake, applying what it could to whisky making. So far the results have been impressive.

TASTING NOTES FOR 12 EIGASHIMA SHUZO WHISKIES

By Yuji Kawasaki

Considering how Eigashima Shuzo only makes whisky a few months out of the year, you can't help but feel it's holding back. However, the distillery is still capable of producing surprisingly elegant and truly excellent whisky.

Akashi White Oak Japanese Blended Whisky 68/100

Young whisky can sometimes feel like the rough texture of wood, here like floorboards left in the sun for a long time. This Akashi is rather hot, too, like a summer day, with some fillet steak spices. The grain whisky is quite strong in this straight shooting blend.

Akashi White Oak Red Japanese Blended Whisky 67/100

The scent of red wood. That's followed by pine, scarlet flowers on the seashore and sawdust. Light and smooth, Akashi Red is balanced but just barely. This budget blend skillfully keeps the grain whisky from becoming unpleasant.

Akashi White Oak

Akashi White Oak Single Malt 76/100

Intense spices. A strong oak note, almost like those big, heavy wooden doors at Japanese whisky bars. This does pack a punch, but it's a dram you'll want to take your time with and, if you smoke, one that might make you hanker for a cigar.

Akashi Zoetrope Private 5 Years Old 87/100

Here "Zoetrope" refers to the Tokyo bar named after Francis Ford Coppola's movie studio and one of the country's few Japanese whisky specialty bars. This private bottling is of a 5-year-old Eigashima single malt.

Akashi Red

White Oak Single Malt Whisky Akashi
8 Years Old

White Oak Single Malt Whisky Akashi
14 Years Old

It's as though the nose on this whisky cuts a core straight through the alcohol. Even though the aroma is robust, the *umami* is well-balanced. The mouthfeel is amazingly moist and sweet. Yet, the way the flavors gradually become increasingly bitter is so smooth you almost don't notice it. The sweetness isn't overbearing but akin to that found in rice cakes stuffed with salted bean jam. Roasted barley rounds out the finish for a bitterness that is characteristic of Eigashima. A grown-up single malt.

Eigashima Japanese Single Malt Whisky Blackadder 87/100

An exceedingly rare single cask Eigashima whisky. The "Blackadder" refers to bottler Blackadder International and this release is limited to a mere 330 bottles.

The nose has grapefruit encompassed by charcoal-like ash. But the ash isn't from some cheap brickett but what's called *bincho-tan* in Japanese,

also known as "white charcoal." Bincho-tan is a high-grade charcoal, so these are elegant ash notes. Taking a sip, sweet citrus is following by warmth. This whisky is like winter in Japan, with the family gathering around a *kotatsu*, a low table covered with a blanket and outfitted with a heater, eating sweet tangerines.

Eigashima Kiri Single Malt Whisky 5 Years Old 68/100

Not Eigashima's best, but these days a more interesting whisky because it was bottled by Gaiaflow, which has now set up its own distillery in Shizuoka. Released in 2015, *kiri* (桐) refers to the paulownia tree, which is where the legendary phoenix perches in folklore and which has become a Japanese governmental symbol. This single malt was first aged in European oak for three years and then finished in a white wine cask for two.

The aromas are fresh, like small blooming flowers in a sunny field.

There's some muscat. Tranquil and unabashedly sweet, you can almost picture a young woman in a white dress playing a harp. A dessert whisky but not much more than that.

Eigashima Single Malt Whisky Sakura 5 Years Old 86/100

Another bottling by Gaiaflow, and perhaps their best Eigashima release. This whisky was aged in a former shochu cask and a hogshead for three years. Then it was finished in a red wine cask for another two. The shochu cask won't have much, if any, influence on flavor but that wine cask certainly does.

Nosing the glass, it smells like brandy. Tasting it, there are raisins, candlesticks, sand, nougat, wheat, fresh cream and *baumkuchen*, the German cake that's beloved in Japan. Not exactly flowery springtime in Japan but still excellent.

Eigashima Kiri Single Malt Whisky 5 Years Old

Eigashima Single Malt Whisky Sakura

White Oak Sea Anchor

Single Malt Whisky Uozumi 76/100

Uozumi is a place in Akashi where Eigashima Shuzo is located, but this single malt certainly doesn't evoke that seaside area. Rather, this is an oil painting depicting a wintery landscape. There's citrus buried in snow. Bricks. A warm fire. You just want to snuggle up on the sofa, unwind and warm yourself with hot honey lemon. The entire experience is somewhat balanced but any blips along the way are overshadowed by the relaxing pace of this whisky.

White Oak Single Malt Whisky Akashi Bourbon Cask 3 Years Old 82/100

The sweetness of this whisky is the first thing that hits. The honey and vanilla notes are followed by freshly toasted bread, maple syrup and even more vanilla. This single malt is a clear, relaxing morning with the sun shining in through the window. It's also further proof that Eigashima's best whiskies aren't blends.

White Oak Sea Anchor 65/100

Of all Eigashima Shuzo's whiskies, this one makes the biggest deal out of its seaside locale. On the nose there's sea water mixed with ash aromas. That's followed by nuts and gentle lemon. The aromas aren't thick but, rather, compact.

Taking a sip, those notes are snuffed out. This whisky certainly needs some of those ash flavors because there's nothing holding it together upon delivery. Lemon, however, does return in the finish. Think of this as a short art house movie—interesting for a few moments but not quite feature film material.

White Oak Single Malt Akashi Sherry Butt 8 Years Old 81/100

The nose is unabashedly sherry. But it's more than that. This single malt just melts in the mouth, and suddenly there's the feeling of summer—sandy beaches and sunburnt skin—and hot days that turn into clear, starry nights, and the feeling that anything is possible, just like a boat heading out on the open sea. Still young, this Akashi wasn't made with the assumption that the general public would appreciate it but whisky fans sure will.

White Oak Single Malt Akashi 14 Years Old 92/100

Here's the result of all the cask experimentation they've been doing at Eigashima Shuzo. Savory charred aromas are exquisitely harmonious with the clear smell of barley and the flavor of Muscat grapes. Eigashima did a superb job with completing the finish in a white wine cask. It isn't only a delicious whisky without complaints but the kind you rarely come across.

NIKKA
YOICHI DISTILLERY

Yoichi is alive with color. Only a few months ago this Hokkaido coastal town and its famed distillery were blanketed in white, with the wind whipping around corners and deep snow turning everything into an ordeal. Now, in front of nearly every house there is a flowerbed with tulips, and inside the Yoichi Distillery the green lawns are covered with yellow dandelions. Gardeners, carrying bamboo brooms and wearing pristine Nikka jumpsuits, start the morning sweeping. Soon, workers in the still house will begin firing the pot stills.

With its heavy stone facade, teal window shutters and pointed red roofs, the Yoichi Distillery looks like it's been plucked from Scotland and airlifted

into a rural Hokkaido, that is, if Scottish distilleries had walkways lined with carefully pruned Japanese yew trees. The distillery, with its stone archway, was supposed to look foreign. Today, it's a portal to another era.

A Town Built on Whisky

During the late 19th century, after Japan underwent a rampant and systematic Westernization process, massive stone and brick buildings went up all over the country, symbolizing change and modernization. These buildings represent excellent whisky. The distillery is famous for its hearty and smoky single malts, winning a slew of international awards and critical praise. It also has a stellar pedigree. Nikka's founder, Masataka

Above Masataka Taketsuru in his later years.
Left Nikka's "king of blenders" is said to be Scottish blender William Phaup Lowrie (1831–1916). His depiction might have been confused with Sir Walter Raleigh as both men's last names are written the same in Japanese (ローリー or "Roorii").
Below Spring tulips bloom all over Yoichi.

Taketsuru, was the first Japanese to go to Scotland and study proper whisky making. With the knowledge he gained, he not only managed the country's first real whisky distillery, Suntory's Yamazaki Distillery, but later went on to establish this one (for more, see pages 20–23).

Even before his time at Yamazaki, Taketsuru thought Hokkaido would be a great place to make whisky. After being demoted to managing a beer brewery, Taketsuru ended his 10-year contract at Kotobukiya (present-day Suntory) in 1934. At nearly 40 he was no spring chicken, and in a work culture that traditionally valued life-time employment, striking out on his own, especially after leaving a giant company like Kotobukiya, was a risk most men would not take. Taketsuru was not most men. But he would not be able to do it by himself. The move would be hardest on his Scottish wife Rita, and if she hadn't agreed to it Nikka Whisky might not have happened.

Near the Yamazaki Distillery sits the former villa of businessman Shotaro

Left In January, the average temperature in Yoichi reaches -4.0 °C (24.8 °F). Walking around town, much less the distillery, is a challenge.
Below Spring is a great time to visit Yoichi. Because the Hokkaido climate is cooler, cherry blossoms bloom later than they do in Osaka and Tokyo.

Kaga. While in Osaka Rita had been teaching his wife English, and the close relationship with that couple would prove instrumental. In the summer of 1934, Kaga would help finance what became Nikka Whisky, and when he passed away he gave all his Nikka stocks to the then president of Asahi Breweries, the company that now owns the whisky maker. The villa, which overlooks the Yamazaki Distillery and belongs to Asahi, is now an art museum as well as a reminder of the complex relationship between Japan's biggest drink makers.

Several locations in Hokkaido were considered for Taketsuru's new distillery, such as Ebetsu, a town close to Sapporo, but was nixed because the area was flood-prone. Yoichi, located on the western coast, eventually won out. Years later, writing in his autobiography, Taketsuru noted how Yoichi's climate and the scenery were reminiscent of Scotland, especially during early morning and dusk. His wife Rita, who was born in Kirkintilloch, also felt at home in Hokkaido. For Taketsuru, this was the best place to make whisky in the entire country.

Compared to Osaka or Tokyo, there are not such drastic changes in weather, from bitter cold to blistering heat. Maturation happens more slowly. Yoichi whiskies take their time. You can taste it.

While the distillery was vital to the town's growth, the area, with its access to local Japanese white oak, peat and coal, had everything Taketsuru needed to make his whisky—even if it wasn't exactly a convenient spot. Yoichi is 839 kilometers (520 miles) from Tokyo and 1,050 kilometers (1,690 miles) from Osaka, the country's biggest markets. To make whisky, this is a terrific location. To ship and sell it in 1930s Japan was impractical.

Hokkaido wasn't settled in earnest by the Japanese until the 19th century. This northern prefecture continues to have a frontier spirit that is similar to the American West, with people coming from all over Japan, trying to make a fresh start, to find success. People with big dreams. People ready to battle long winters. People like the Taketsurus.

The Nikka Difference

"There are several key differences between how we make whisky here and how whisky is made in Scotland,"

Left Initially Taketsuru could only afford one still, which had to be cleaned out between the first and second distillations, making the process even more laborious.
Below More stills were added in the years that followed. Note the Shinto garlands draped around the neck of each.
Bottom An archival photo showing a horse-drawn cart carrying whisky casks making its way down the distillery's main drag.

says distillery manager Koichi Nishikawa, who previously headed up the Ben Nevis distillery in Scotland, which Nikka also owns. "One of the biggest differences is the huge turnover of distillery workers," Nishikawa continues. "People were always coming and going in Scotland. That doesn't happen here in Japan. Most people who join this distillery spend their entire careers here."

This means there's continuity, but it doesn't mean things remain unchanged. Nikka is continually tweaking its process to make better whisky. What it also means is that at Nikka, and in the Japanese whisky industry in general, there simply isn't a flow of labor between companies. This also might mean there is a greater sense of responsibility among the long-time Nikka workers. Nishikawa explained that it was sometimes harder to pinpoint when things went pear-shaped in Scotland. "I remember once at Ben Nevis the entire fermentation tank was accidentally drained. I asked the person in charge and he just wouldn't tell me what happened. No one would. That simply would not happen here at Yoichi." While the Japanese might have a deeper sense of duty, Nishikawa believes the Scottish industry has a stronger adherence to tradition than the Japanese one.

"In Scotland there seemed to be a greater desire to keep and protect tradition because it was tradition," Nishikawa says. "In Japan we are more willing to try new things. We'll protect what works and change things that don't." This isn't only true in the whisky business. This willingness to change and be flexible is evident

Right The original Super Nikka was bottled in hand-blown Kagami Crystal, the glass-ware of the Japanese Imperial Household. Nikka released about 1,000 bottles a year until 1970, but has since released reasonably priced Super Nikka revivals which don't come in crystal bottles.

Center right Before Nikka got into the whisky business, it was in the apple juice business.

Far right The prestigious World Whisky Awards named Yoichi Distillery's Koichi Nishikawa Distillery Manager of the Year for 2016.

Below right Northland (middle, green bottle) is the first Japanese whisky to be done in a true Scottish blend style—malt whiskies from different domestic distilleries blended with grain whisky.

throughout the country's history. It's how the Japanese language developed, how its clothing changed and how its diet evolved. The most Japanese thing about Japan is its willingness to discard what it no longer needs and to select what it wants to keep. Outside forces might be acting on the country to induce change, but ultimately it's the Japanese who make the final call. This can be seen at Nikka. There is this notion that Nikka's founder, Masataka Taketsuru, was dogmatic about his desire to make a true Scotch-style whisky. That he stormed off to Hokkaido to do just that. The reality is that Taketsuru was a pragmatic businessman, willing to experiment and to abandon what didn't work.

Taketsuru's venture was originally called Dai Nippon Kaju (Great Japan Fruit Juice), but as with so many long names in Japanese, the title was soon

shortened to Nikka. Before the company got its distiller's license, it produced apple juice. At the time, the decision might've made sense because Taketsuru needed something to sell before his whisky business was up and running. After the importation of American seedlings, Yoichi was one of the first places where apples were cultivated in Japan during the 1870s. Taketsuru knew about making sake and whisky, but apple juice? He was a novice. To complicate things, Dai Nippon Kaju's aim was additive-free apple juice at a time when products such as that were still novel. The real deal was too cloudy for Japanese customers who weren't used to drinking all natural juice and were unhappy that the flavor and color could change depending on the season. At that time the juice market, like the whisky one, was flooded with

imitations. While Taketsuru tried marketing his apple juice as a health beverage, even selling it to hospitals, it was twice as expensive as the era's popular soft drinks, such as the fizzy soda pop known as *ramune*. The apple juice venture was a failure.

But Taketsuru didn't travel all the way to Hokkaido to only make apple juice. In 1936, Nikka got its first pot still, shipped from Watanabe Iron Works in Osaka. Even though the young distillery could only afford one still, meaning that the still had to be painstakingly cleaned out in between distillations, Taketsuru refocused on whisky. But he didn't give up on apples. During his lifetime he tried releasing a whole array of apple-related products, ranging from the successful apple brandy, which is still available today, to the less successful apple ketchup, which, thankfully, is not.

Memories of Master Massan

"I was 14 years old when Nikka hired me, and the smallest worker at the distillery," says Tatsujiro Shimamiya, now in his late eighties. He sits on a tatami mat at the Yoichi Cafe, flipping through old photos with another Nikka vet, Takeshi Aoki. Shimamiya takes a sip of coffee. "Here I am," he says, pointing to a scrawny kid in a group photo in front of the Yoichi Distillery's wooden office. Front and center is Masataka Taketsuru.

It was 1943. With the men off fighting and with Nikka's distillery designated part of the war effort, Nikka brought in women and teenagers to distill its whisky and continue production. It wasn't only churning out whisky for the imperial troops but also making wine because a by-product was tartaric acid, which was used by the military to manufacture radars. It was a different era, with the notion that junior high school students working in factories was hardly unusual.

"When I was hired, I was assigned to work in the office," Shimamiya says. "But I wanted to work in the still house." It wasn't because he liked whisky, he was just a kid, but because he thought it was cooler than, for example, bringing paperwork to the bank. He takes another

sip of coffee and adds with a chuckle, "I've never really ever drunk whisky."

That first day, Taketsuru came over to a young Shimamiya and said in his big, booming voice that he should buck up and do his best. "I remember thinking, 'Is this man Japanese?'" Shimamiya says. "He sure didn't seem Japanese." Taketsuru was short, but he was strong and stocky thanks to years of judo practice. He seemed larger than life. "Taketsuru-san had this huge presence and huge moustache," says Yoichi native Aoki, who joined Nikka in the 1960s and whose mother worked on the bottling line. "When he would come around the distillery, I couldn't make eye contact with him."

Driven and strict, Taketsuru was incredibly punctual and very particular about the food he ate. He pushed himself hard and expected the same from his employees. "He never beat around the

Above Tatsujiro Shimamiya looking through old photos at the Yoichi Cafe.
Below In this staff photo from April 1944, a young Shimamiya is in the third row, fifth from the right. He is the smallest one in the photo. Save for management, the distillery workers were either boys too young to fight or were women.

bush," says Shimamiya, "and would always tell you exactly what he was thinking." But Taketsuru also loved playing sports and games with his staff, whether it was baseball or volleyball, or even mah-jong well into the evening. He had a good sense of humor and would joke how he knew the distillery workers kept sneaking sips of whisky. No doubt some were.

At the age of 15, after a year of running office errands, Shimamiya was finally assigned to the still house where he would distill whisky for the next 20 years. "When I started, women were also working the stills and shoveling coal," Shimamiya says. "Now, it's not as difficult to fire the stills because the coal is good quality. But during the war it was like sand, so keeping the fires hot and the stills going was hard." After the war, when the troops returned from fighting, the still house once again became a male preserve. In recent years that has changed, but it's not the only thing that has.

"Now at Yoichi, whisky is only distilled twice and the casks are filled at 63 percent alcohol," Shimamiya recalls. "But when I started, we were distilling three times and filling strength was 70 percent alcohol." According to Shimamiya, the first still was made of cast iron and shaped like the other stills at Yoichi, but was behind

a partition. This was not because the distillery was hiding anything from visitors (because, at that time there were no crowds of tourists pouring into the distillery like today), but perhaps, because the distillery didn't want the secret police to confiscate the iron and melt it down for the war effort.

After the first distillation in the iron still, Shimamiya says, the spirit was then double distilled in two copper pot stills. By the 1960s this practice seems to have been phased out, and Yoichi was distilling its whisky twice, just like other Japanese malt whisky makers. The vast majority of Scotch is double distilled, unlike Irish whisky which is generally distilled three times. But there are a handful of Scotch whiskies that are triple distilled, such as Hazelburn, where Taketsuru apprenticed briefly while in Scotland, so perhaps this is why Shimamiya says whisky was originally distilled three times at Yoichi. It could have also been a way for Nikka to get a smoother, higher proof spirit.

Yoichi might've been a wartime factory but it was run by an English-speaking man who not only had been educated abroad but had married a Scottish-born woman called Rita Cowan. "She spoke beautiful Japanese," Shimamiya says. Even though she had become a naturalized Japanese, rumors still persisted. The distillery was never bombed by the Allies, though it almost was on several occasions. Gossip swirled that the antenna on the Taketsuru's house was sending messages to the Allies or that Rita would wave her hanky, telling planes overhead not to bomb the distillery. "Before Nikka became part of the war effort," Aoki says, "there are stories that the *kempeitai*, the military's secret police, was always watching to see if Rita was a spy or if there were spies at the distillery."

Right An older Taketsuru relaxes on a bridge.
Below Rita left her mark on Yoichi. Those who knew her still remember her fondly. The town's main street is called Rita Road and its Christian nursery school, Rita Yochien (Rita Kindergarten), now bears her name.

Shimamiya dismisses the rumors, saying, "These were the Americans, right? They probably had aerial photos and maps and knew it was a whisky distillery. Besides, Americans wouldn't blow up a whisky distillery." As the war raged on, Rita went outside less and less. Imagine the conflicting feelings that Taketsuru, a man who had dedicated most of his life to learning about the English-speaking world, had seeing his country dub the United Kingdom as the enemy. Imagine how Rita must have felt.

"After the war ended, most of the other school kids quit but I stayed on," Shimamiya said. He worked for the distillery for decades, staying connected to the company long after he stopped making whisky. He recalls the generosity Taketsuru showed him and his family, offering him rides home in the company car, an unusual gesture for a corporate honcho. Taketsuru even asked a grown Shimamiya and his family to live in his Yoichi residence for five years when he was in Tokyo overseeing the company's expansion. The house has since been moved to the distillery grounds. "I get all sorts of memories when I pass it," Shimamiya says. As a little boy, Aoki remembers snooping around and peeking in the kitchen window to watch Rita make oxtail soup. "I had never seen or smelled anything like it," he says. Taketsuru shared the house with his wife Rita until she passed away in 1961.

After Rita's death, Taketsuru threw himself into his work like never before. For years Nikka produced solid, well-crafted whiskies but Taketsuru knew he could do better. The result was the deliciously sherried Super Nikka, released the following year. Priced at 3,000 yen, it was one of the most expensive whiskies available. At that time the average salary for a newly hired university grad was 21,000 yen a month! "Super Nikka gave him confidence, I think," Shimamiya says. "He knew that he had finally made a great whisky that could not be beaten."

Above It's still possible to find Yoichi single malts with aged statements at some bars, but they started vanishing from stores in 2014. With time, they'll return.

Right A peek inside Yoichi's mash tun. The distillery uses both peated and unpeated imported malted barley.

fermentation span in the future but adds that the current process produces a deep, heavy wash. "I don't think you can say five days of fermentation is better than three," he continues. "You just end up with a different style of wash and that carries over into the distilled spirit. The newly distilled spirit we are currently getting is very fragrant." This is just one of the ways Nikka continues to tune its whiskies.

Fired by Coal

"This is the first still," Koyano says, pointing. Above the furnace there is a plaque commemorating this fact. When the Yoichi Distillery first started distilling whisky in 1936, Taketsuru was only able to afford one still until a second was added in 1940. The still house is now filled with a row of them. All are a deep reddish brown, save for a glimmering pot refurbished by Miyake Industries in late 2015. Today, that still is silent, but nearby 43-year-old Shouji Namioka shovels coal. A fire under the massive pot still crackles and sizzles, while above the still creaks and squeaks as a series of copper chains called the rummager slowly turn inside to prevent charring and adding even more flavor to the spirit. Wearing a hard hat, clear plastic visor and surgical mask, Namioka works quickly and precisely, not dropping a single lump of coal as he attends to the flames.

Yoichi is the only distillery in the world that still uses coal. It's always been that way here since the 1930s. Even Scotland has long moved on to easier, more economical ways to make their whisky. Coal requires tough manual labor and constant attention,

The Fragrant Aromas of Yoichi

Decked out in a Nikka helmet and blue and white workware, Yoshikazu Koyano strides through the distillery carrying a clipboard. To every visitor that passes by—and it's a seemingly endless stream of them—he bows his head ever so slightly, wishing them a good day. Koyano, who works in the General Affairs Section, pushes open the door to the Mill Room. "This probably doesn't suit Yoichi like the old mill we used until 2011," says Koyano, pointing up to a compact German machine that replaced the huge Japanese-made one that used to occupy much of this room. "But it sure does make our life easier." Likewise, the mill isn't milling Japanese barley any more because Nikka, like many of its competitors rely on imports.

The milled barley is then mixed with hot water in the mash tun and the whole room smells like warm oatmeal. The resulting wort is piped over with yeast starter called *shubo* to the next building into the fermentation tanks. With Taketsuru's sake-family background, it makes sense that shubo, a sake-yeasting technique, is used at Yoichi (for more on shubo, see page 30). Even though the tanks are stainless steel and sealed shut, the faint aroma of milky apples tickles the nose.

"Now, we ferment the wort for five days," says Koyano. "In the past we fermented it for three days, like other distilleries in Japan and Scotland, but about ten years ago we began doing it for five days." Koyano points out that the Yoichi Distillery might change this but it produces delicious whisky. Today, most Scottish distilleries heat their pot stills with steam coils, while a handful, such as Glenfarclas, directly fire their stills with gas-powered flames. In the past, the way most Scotch whisky makers heated their pot stills was coal, which remained common in Scotland during the 1970s. But by the 1990s, distilleries were switching over to steam coils. It wasn't until 2005 that Glendronach, the last Scottish distillery to fire its stills with coal, switched to indirect steam heating to comply with tough European Union regulations.

From the late 19th century and into the first half of the 20th, coal mining was a major industry in Japan. The idea that Japan has been without natural resources is incorrect. Modernization and wars led the country into using much of them. When Taketsuru picked Hokkaido, he knew he could easily secure the rock, but in the years after World War II, production dropped and cheaper foreign imports increased. By the mid-1970s, Nikka was importing Australian coal. But why does this distillery stick with the black fuel? Unlike steam-fired or gas-fired stills, using coal causes fluctuations in temperature in the distillate and the smoke from the coal also gives another layer of flavors. "The result is a more complex and robust spirit with a lot of character," explains distillery manager Koichi Nishikawa. "These coal-fired stills are one of the things that makes the Yoichi Distillery unique." And,

without a doubt, its whiskies great.

"This is something we have to do by hand," Namioka says, after finishing his shovel of coal. "But it is hard work." Beads of sweat roll down the side of his cheeks. In less than ten minutes he'll need to tend to the fires. In the meantime, he heads into a small office at the opposite end of the still house. Even though he wears heavy gloves while working, his hands are still smudged with coal. The nearby sink is cluttered with several types of soap. Inside the office, there's a desktop PC and a monitor showing a schematic of all the stills, allowing Namioka to track their temperature. He twists open a bottle of water. "We're aiming for 92 °C [198 °F]," he says, taking a sip. The goal is to keep it under 100 °C [212 °F], the boiling point of water. This is dangerous work, and a laminated printout in the office warns workers to wear the long-sleeved work uniform to protect against flames.

To keep the temperature constant, every seven or eight minutes Namioka

Left Coal must be shoveled every seven or eight minutes to keep the fire at the desired temperature.
Below Since coal fires fluctuate, the resulting distillate has added character.

must tend to each fire, adding three more shovels of coal. Today, only two stills are in operation, but when more are distilling Namioka's workdays are even busier. "We start firing the stills at 9 am in the morning and finish at 4 pm," he says. Summers are dreadfully hot, but it's easier to start the fire in the morning, while winters make the still house an ideal place to be, even if it's harder to get the fire going on those cold mornings. "All this effort is worth it," Namioka explains. "You can taste it in the whisky."

Inside, the still house is smoky. Stepping outside, no clouds puff from the chimney as they did in years past, which is why some older Yoichi locals don't think the distillery is making whisky! "We added layers and layers of filtering in the chimney," says Nishikawa. "It's necessary and helps keep the air clean."

Protection of the Gods

Shinto garlands called *shimenawa* are draped around each still. Garlands like these are found at Shinto shrines to mark holy areas and to ward off evil spirits. They are also wrapped around rocks and trees that are believed to be *yorishiro* or rod-like objects that *kami* or spirits are able to enter. Even though Shintoism has a strong connection to alcohol, namely sake, shimenawa wrapped around the stills are more for protection than for marking them as divine lightning rods. Fire and high-proof alcohol can make for a danger-ous combination, as evident by a Yoichi

Traditionally in Japan, alcohol production has had a close relationship with Shintoism.

Distillery fire in the 1940s which destroyed the then wooden still house, but thankfully left the stills intact.

Each January, right after the distillery workers get back from their extended New Year's holidays, a Shinto priest comes to Yoichi and blesses the stills and prays for safety. In Japan, it's not uncommon for Shinto priests to do this for any number of things. Cars, for example, get blessed to help prevent accidents, and there's even one shrine near Tokyo's geek and electronics center of Akihabara that will bless people's computers so they don't break down! Nothing is left to chance. The distillery has a laundry list of practical safety precautions to keep its workers safe. The blessings are more to ward off any unforeseen evil and accidents.

A Shinto garland is also draped over the doorway of the distillery's first maturation warehouse. Since that warehouse is largely for tourists and because it doesn't actually store whisky (rather, it's part of the distillery's museum tour), the garlands there are

less for safety and more to mark the warehouse as sacred ground. However, the maturation warehouses where whisky is aged do not have garlands draped over their entrances.

Throughout her life, Rita was a devout Christian and active in her local church. Shortly before Taketsuru passed away in 1979, he converted to Christianity, and the tomb they share is inscribed with a large cross. Typically, Buddhist priests preform funeral rites in Japan but Taketsuru's conversation ensured that he would be buried with Rita in a Christian grave. However, for most Japanese, Taketsuru included, Shintoism isn't something that can be separated from other religions or, for that matter, separated from Japan. Perhaps he felt he needed the Shinto gods, with their long-standing connection to alcohol, right up until the end.

Japanese Whisky, American Oak

Outside there's a huge, green lawn. During the 1950s and 1960s, distillery workers would come here during their lunch breaks. They'd eat as fast as they could so that they could spend the remaining time playing pick-up games of baseball or volleyball. Walking along the edge of the field, the now-quiet bottling plant is to the immediate right. All Yoichi whisky used to be bottled on-site but now it's done at Nikka's Kashiwa plant, outside Tokyo. On the opposite side of the field is the cooperage where casks are refurbished and repaired.

The Miyagikyo Distillery

Completed in 1969, Nikka's second malt distillery is in Miyagi Prefecture. Nikka founder Masataka Taketsuru had two prerequisites for the location. First, it had to be further south than the Yoichi Distillery, and second, it needed a good water source. The city of Sendai had just the spot, right off the seemingly fated Nikkawa River. The Sendai Distillery—later, Miyagikyo—was thus born.

The Miyagikyo Distillery's whiskies are often compared to a Lowland style of Scotch, having softer notes that contrast with the Yoichi Distillery's heavier, smokier whiskies. "At Yoichi, the pot stills are small and squat and they are direct-fired by coal," says Nikka's chief blender Tadashi Sakuma. "However, the Miyagikyo pot stills are much larger and taller, so you get a crisper, more floral spirit." Since Japanese distilleries traditionally don't trade whiskies, having a second distillery with a different profile gives blenders a wider palette. "Yoichi and Miyagikyo are obviously different," says Sakuma. "So even if you do the exact same thing, the results won't be."

The Miyagikyo Distillery is also home to Nikka's Coffey still, named after the Irish inventor Aeneas Coffey who patented a two-column style of continuous still. Taketsuru first learned how grain whisky was distilled in Coffey Stills during his 1919 apprenticeship at Bo'ness in Scotland. Decades later, in 1963, Taketsuru imported a Coffey still from Scotland and housed it at Nikka's Nishinomiya Distillery outside Kobe, but later moved it to the Miyagikyo Distillery where it continues to produce high-grade spirit. Using this old still does give the distillate special characteristics, but what's most unusual is Nikka's decision to produce a 100 percent malt whisky via the Coffey Still—something not traditionally done in Scotland.

Above Taketsuru's concept was that Yoichi would serve as Nikka's robust Highland-style distillery, while Miyagikyo would be the milder Lowland-style one.
Right The cooperage at Miyagikyo refurbishes casks and makes new ones. Empty casks are left outside to prevent them from drying out.
Far right Miyagikyo's towering steam-fired pot stills have boil-balls and are taller than the squat Yoichi pot stills with their lyne arms angling up. The result is a lighter spirit.

"Okay, let's char it," says cooper Kazuyuki Shoji. He gestures to the cask and one of the other coopers, a young, fresh-faced kid, who rolls a 250-liter (66-gallon) hogshead onto a short platform. He presses a button and the burner, a long contraption with snake-like pipes, fires a steady blue flame. It sounds like a jet plane taking off. The inside of the cask is ablaze and flames shoot into the air. The cask is continuously rotated, ensuring an even char. The burner shuts off and squirts water into the burning cask, extinguishing the flames. Once the machine finishes and the fire is put out, a cooper gently rolls the cask down to the floor of the cooperage and sprays the inside with a hose. "Here, stick your nose in and take a whiff," says Shoji. It smells delicious, like a hot vanilla latte drizzled with honey. "This cask is made from American white oak," Shoji says.

"We used to use Japanese *mizunara* when this distillery first started, but they leak, so now American white oak is most common." Sherry casks are also used, but chief blender Tadashi Sakuma says American white oak probably best suits Yoichi.

"Originally, we aged our whisky in new casks," says Sakuma. But in the decades after World War II, with inexpensive and sturdy bourbon barrels widely available, making new casks became less common or even necessary for Nikka. "We did realize that cask-making is impor-

tant," Sakuma says. Not only do new casks impart different characteristics on the spirit, making casks is part of a long-standing tradition. "To ensure that we at Nikka could continue to make our own casks, we brought in the apprentices of master cooper Yoshiro Komatsuzaki to show the younger coopers at Nikka how to make new casks and carry on that tradition." During the 1990s Nikka made a small number of new casks in-house but it wasn't until 2000 that it began producing them in earnest. New casks made at Nikka's cooperage at

Miyagikyo now comprise about 10 percent of all its stock.

"We also take care of our casks," Shoji says. "We want to use them for as long as we can. That's our responsibility. And if you do that, you can use them much longer than we'll be alive." At 49 years old, Shoji is the eldest of the three coopers working today. The other two are decades younger. "The old Japanese style of just watching and learning is no good," says Shoji. "Younger craftsmen need to do things themselves, and while they're doing it they watch and learn. That's the best

way." Shoji picks up a cask head and puts it on a metal table where he begins charring it by hand. "The younger coopers can take what I say and use what works," he continues. "They can disregard what doesn't. Then, they'll pass that information down to the next generation, who will make their own decisions on what to keep and what not to." This way of thinking, about keeping what works and ditching what doesn't, permeates the distillery.

One of the younger coopers begins sealing a cask. He takes a dried strip of river reed, wets it and then puts it

Far left Flames shoot out of a cask as a torch chars the cask. There are different degrees of charring—light, medium and heavy. At Yoichi, casks get either a medium or heavy char.

Above left Stacks of cask heads (lids) at the Yoichi cooperage. These American oak heads were made at the Miyagikyo cooperage and are stamped "Sendai."

Above center A cooper seals a cask with a river reed to prevent leaking.

Above right The fire in a freshly charred cask is extinguished with water.

Left Charring not only unlocks flavors and aromas in the wood but also creates a layer of charcoal that filters out the spirit's unpleasant compounds during the interaction between wood and whisky. Here, both a cask head and a cask are being charred.

What Japanese Whisky Means

"Recently, the phrase 'Japanese whisky' is being used more and more," says Nikka chief blender Tadashi Sakuma, "but I don't think it has much meaning." Rain drizzles down the window and Sakuma is in a second-floor meeting room of Nikka's Kashiwa bottling plant, located a short train ride from Tokyo. This is also where Nikka blenders concoct the company's award-winning whiskies.

Sakuma, who joined Nikka in 1982, initially at the Yoichi Distillery, is refreshingly frank. He quickly says that even as chief blender he doesn't possess any special smelling abilities, didn't get any certification or go through any specialized training. "It was more like the Nikka bigwigs said, 'Let's go with that guy,'" Sakuma says, chuckling. Instead, he chalks up blending to experience. "If you did it every day, you'd figure it out, too," he quips. Whether or not one could ever blend as well as Sakuma is another matter. "What blending needs is experi-

ence and patience," he says. "Whiskies can be blended an infinite number of ways. The job of the blender is to find out what works and what doesn't."

Whatever Nikka is doing, it's working, and working well. Nikka continues to rack up awards and praise for its malts and blends. Sakuma might think Nikka's whisky is special but he isn't quite sold on the notion that Japanese whisky and Scotch whisky are totally different. "Our founder went to Scotland, learned the country's way of making whisky and brought that back to Japan as is," he says, adding that if you put a Nikka whisky into a Scotch blind tasting he doesn't think people would be able to pick it out as Japanese. "Of course," Sakuma says, "Japanese influences exist but I don't think it's completely different, not like bourbon. Instead, Scotch whisky and Japanese whisky are like the same word but maybe the pronunciation is different." So think, "whisky" versus "uisukii."

Yet, Nikka doesn't make whisky exactly like Scottish distilleries do. It uses a wider variety of yeast strains than Scottish distilleries, which, Sakuma points out, typically only use two strains. Nikka also uses virgin (new) American white oak, while in Scotland there's been more aversion to the practice because of fears that the wood will overwhelm the spirit. Nikka also produces a malt whisky via Coffey Still, which, as previously noted, isn't traditionally done in Scotland.

While Sakuma might have been quick to shut down any idea of Japanese whisky being different, he does concede that the approach and thinking are not the same. "To put it simply, there are over a hundred distilleries in Scotland," Sakuma says. "They just need to keep the flavors they've always had." The goal, he explains, is to preserve because what they already have is so good. There's no reason to improve. "We're not like that at Nikka," he says. "We're not preserving our flavors but improving

Far left Chief blender Tadashi Sakuma noses a whisky in the blenders' lab. Like Nikka founder Masataka Taketsuru, Sakuma wears a white lab coat. He measures out small amounts from Yoichi or Miyagikyo samples with a pipette dropper, placing them in a glass when concocting blends.

Left Kashiwa is in Chiba Prefecture, outside Tokyo. The plant is not open to the public.

Below Sakuma must make regular trips to Miyagikyo and Yoichi (pictured) to check the stock.

around the edges of the head as he closes the cask, making a tight seal. Dried river reed strips hang from the cooperage's ceiling. "We took those reeds from around here," Shoji points out. If necessary, the river reed stripes can also be inserted between staves to plug up leaks. "If the staves themselves or the head are leaking, then we take a piece of bamboo, drive that into the wood, which causes the grain to spread and tighten, thereby stopping the leak. Bamboo is light, easy to work with and doesn't leak." After the cask is sealed, it's taken into an adjacent room where it's filled with water and left overnight to see if it leaks. If not, it's then filled with whisky. "Whisky and water are different, obviously, so after that we still need to check it."

them." The reason for that, he says, goes back to the birth of Japanese whisky.

"When our founder established that first distillery, he wasn't able to successfully create the flavors of Scotch-style whisky," he says. "Even though we now have nearly a hundred years of whisky-making know-how and our distillery equipment is the same, we might think that what we are making isn't as good as Scotch."

Sakuma pauses, momentarily. "But, that's no way to think," he says. "So, at Nikka it's ingrained into everyone that we need to make whisky that is better than Scotch. That's why, if we change things, then we can make even more delicious whisky. Perhaps, that is the difference with Japanese whisky." Perhaps it is.

Yoichi's Traditional Warehouses

The sky is gray and it could rain any minute. The coopers are working quickly. They load filled casks for the forklift to carry to one of 26 Yoichi warehouses. Only four of them are rack style while the rest are dunnage warehouses with dirt floors and casks stacked two high. Dunnage warehouses are the traditional way whisky was aged in Scotland but they take up more land because whisky is only stacked a few casks high. Many aficionados swear by dunnage warehouses, saying they result in a better whisky, thanks to a more stable maturation environment and even more interaction with the micro-climate.

In the decades following World War II, Scottish distilleries increasingly began using racked-style warehouses, allowing them to fill casks in economical, multi-story concrete buildings on

iron racks. Also, they're more efficient laborwise. Getting casks out of dunnage warehouses can take twice as long because getting whisky off the upper planks isn't only time-consuming but even more dangerous than rolling them onto a racked warehouse's elevator. Excellent Japanese whisky is aged in dunnage and racked style warehouses and some distilleries, such as Yoichi, have both.

Outside, the air smells of rain but stepping inside one of those dunnage warehouses at Yoichi there's a soft, rich earthy sweetness. It couldn't be more different from the smokiness of the still house. The building is slate but the floor is earth. Inside there's wood paneling for extra insulation and low-hanging wood rafters. Yet, the windows are thin and light streams in through a doorway at the opposite end.

The door to the warehouse shuts. The coopers have finished loading up the casks as rain begins to fall. Across the field, inside the still house, there's a few more shovels of coal before distillation ends for the day. But don't look for those coal-fired stills to go silent any time soon. Says distillery manager Koichi Nishikawa, "We're going to keep using coal to make our whisky as long as we can."

Left Yoichi has 26 warehouses on-site, aging fewer than 5,000 casks. Four of the warehouses are racked while the rest are dunnage style like this. The casks are stacked only two high, which isn't the most economical use of space. That, however, isn't the point.

Below Yoichi aging warehouses are blanketed with snow on a chilly January night. Inside, whisky slowly matures in oak casks.

TASTING NOTES FOR 28 NIKKA WHISKIES

By Yuji Kawasaki

Nikka makes a range of whiskies from inexpensive to anything but. Its Yoichi and Miyagikyo distilleries produce some of the most flavorful spirits in Japan—and the world. Yoichi's single malts are hefty and sturdy, with distinctive coal smoke flavors. Miyagikyo, in contrast, makes floral single malts that open up like fields of flowers. Its best blends are not only well crafted and delicious but are often available at reasonable prices.

Black Nikka Blender's Spirit 60th Anniversary Bottled in 2016 85/100

Deep, fragrant forest aromas are followed up by oak and honey. You lean in further and it's almost like you can hear footsteps down a worn trail in summertime.

The cask notes on this whisky are exceedingly well balanced and they carry through on that first sip. This is a young, budget-priced blend, but why doesn't the wood come off as cheap? There are four or five layers of sweetness and bitterness that seem to float in and out, alternating between them. Black Nikka Blenders Spirit is a carpenter's table made from young wood. The lumber is fresh but the craftsmanship is practiced and honed.

Black Nikka Clear Blend 56/100

Right off the bat you're greeted with delicious warm cereal notes and sweet scents from the cask. There's a charred aroma that grabs hold of your nose and doesn't let go. Black Nikka Clear has a mellow arrival, followed by a banquet of malt and grain. Noticeably, there's the distinctly mild taste of iron.

Black Nikka Rich Blend 67/100

Another Japanese convenience store whisky and one of the best of that ilk.

The bottle points out that this is a whisky with a "rich and well-balanced taste for the casual whisky enthusiast." It has aromas of sweet strawberries, honey, barley and scorched cornhusks. Taking a sip, the taste of freshly cut barley come to the forefront. There are also big oaky flavors and even metallic ones. But, by the second sip, you already start to lose interest.

Black Nikka Blender's Spirit

Miyagikyo Single Malt (No Age Statement) 81/100

Along with the Yoichi single malt line-up, Miyagikyo single malts began vanishing from store shelves. By fall 2015 Nikka had little choice but to retool and release only Miyagikyo and Yoichi single malts without age statements. The Miyagikyo release isn't as good as the Yoichi one, but considering how Nikka was caught off-guard with the sudden demand and decreasing stock, it is well put together.

On the nose, the aroma of unripe strawberries brings expectations of sweet and sour, but instead it's rose thorns and faint smoke for an experience that's reminiscent of hazy sunlight in a gloomy sky. Thinly spread chocolate and a teeny bit of strawberry do put in an appearance.

Miyagikyo Single Malt 10 Years Old 85/100

It's like a bushel of flowers wrapped in barley. The delivery is smooth and light. However, it builds to a long and powerful finish, like those last lingering days of August. Another refreshing Nikka whisky that's good any time of the year!

Miyagikyo Single Malt (No Age Statement)

Miyagikyo Single Malt 10 Years Old, Miyagikyo Single Malt 12 Years Old and Miyagikyo Single Malt 15 Years Old

Miyagikyo Single Malt 12 Years Old 85/100

Bunches of berries, green leaves and colorful flowers. In the background concrete, hot asphalt and paint thinner notes are present. A dram evocative of Japan's picturesque rural roads and the breezy, cool tunnels that make their way through the mountains. Relaxing and serene.

Miyagikyo Single Malt 15 Years Old 87/100

Another flowery Miyagikyo malt. Nosing the glass, it's like a bouquet of flowers was chucked out of the glass directly in your face. There's also some light smoke, adding a layer of refinement. Tasting the whisky, the malted cereal is packed with fruity floral flavors for a satisfying experience.

Nikka From the Barrel 86/100

Nikka took unpeated malt and aged grain whisky and blended them, but instead of bottling them at that point Nikka put them in casks for further maturation for another 3–6 months with the idea of making even more

harmonious aromas and flavors. In the whisky business this is called "marrying." The resulting whisky is fairly close to cask strength and bottled at a slightly lower 51.4 percent abv.

As with whiskies of this strength, the alcohol is noticeable. But behind that the aromas are sweet and fresh with lovely raspberry notes. In the background there are also old books and burnt wood. The delivery is quite smooth but this blend makes a vividly clear, passionate statement. It is one of the best affordable grown-up whiskies in Japan—and the world.

Nikka Single Malt 23 Years Old Yoichi 88/100

Fragrant notes of sea breeze and wet sand are mixed with crisp, freshly cut pine. There's the hint of a sweet aroma. The palette is cool and refreshing like a watermelon, evoking long summer evenings. This expression is a distillery bottling and sadly not for sale.

The Nikka 12 Years Old 87/100

Whenever Nikka puts the definite article "The" on a whisky, you get the

feeling the maker has confidence in it, and each time those whiskies are lavished with praise. What about this 12-year-old? It's the youngest The Nikka and certainly smells sweetly sublime, like burnt honey that was cooled with water. In the background there is refreshing orange aromas, which come through on the palette and coat charred oak flavors in a thin citrus veil.

The Nikka 40 Years Old 98/100

This is a whisky that Nikka has thrown its full might behind. It's a limited edition blended bottling to mark the maker's 80th anniversary that contains Yoichi distilled whisky dating from 1945, when World War II ended, as well as Miyagikyo distilled whisky dating from 1969 when that distillery opened in Sendai.

The result is a beautiful symphony. It's oaky, fruity and quite crisp, with hints of the kind of smoke you get from sparklers in summertime. The arrival makes for a wonderous feeling as if you are drinking several distinct whiskies at the same time. It's actually

Nikka From the Barrel

The Nikka 40 Years Old

Taketsuru Pure Malt 12 Years Old

like listening to an orchestra where you can pick out each member of the ensemble the moment that they play. The one common note that is a hit throughout the entire experience is the Yoichi Distillery's signature spiciness, providing added force. In a single instant, this is both Nikka's past and its future. This is a whisky that's just about perfect.

The Nikka Whisky 1998 34 Years Old 98/100

The aromas on this Nikka leap far past "pleasant." The aroma is as if a sherry cask were bottled and sold as perfume. The wood notes are warm and there is the smell of finely sliced high-quality ham. All sorts of memories come rushing forth, and it's easy to feel you'd like to get intoxicated just by nosing this whisky.

Nice, soft mouthfeel, but at the same time you're acutely aware of how it feels on the tongue, and the elegantly aged wood and floral aromas go right to your nose for a whisky with both dignity and grace.

The Nikka Whisky 1999 34 Years Old 98/100

Here we have another 34-year-old single malt from Nikka. This one, however, is from 1999. What makes this whisky so fascinating is how it stacks up against its 1998 brethren.

A thick, enrapturing aroma on this one, with nuances of metal chains, stones and mulch. Underneath a slightly acidic scent lurk floral notes, both in the scent of blooming flowers and the smell of a dried bouquet. There's Japanese incense as well as a chalky note that is reminiscent of the lime powder used on baseball fields.

The arrival is so poised that it's surprising. Even though the finish is so heavy and so spicy, delicate aromas linger until you exhale. It's complex and multi-layered *umami* savoriness. With this one, you can't fall back on the standard explanations for a whisky matured in sherry casks, such as sweet or astringent. The experience is much more than that.

Rare Old Black Nikka Whisky 86/100

A contemporary re-release of the classic Black Nikka, which originally came out in 1956. It's a straight forward, no nonsense whisky. You get lots of barley on the nose and some faint smoke. That follows through on the arrival, while it's as though the sweetness of the sugary wort is concentrated and perfected in the final whisky. Delightful.

Super Nikka Whisky (First Revival Version) 86/100

Released in the wake of the popular NHK drama *Massan* about Masataka Taketsuru and his wife Rita, this 2015 "reprint" edition aims to let modern whisky fans try a modern re-creation of the original Super Nikka Whisky expression released in 1962.

Gently swirl the glass and barley asserts itself in the middle of sweet aromas. Is that a slightly toasted note on the barley? It's a smooth, creamy easy-to-drink whisky that seems to coat the inside of your mouth before a mellow yet smoky finish.

Taketsuru Pure Malt 17 Years Old, Taketsuru Pure Malt 21 Years Old and Taketsuru Pure Malt Non-Chill Filtered 21 Years Old.

Taketsuru Pure Malt 25 Years Old

Yoichi Single Malt 10 Years Old

Taketsuru Pure Malt (No Age Statement) 88/100

"Taketsuru" refers to the founder of Nikka Whisky, commonly known as "The Father of Japanese Whisky." With the increasing demand for whisky, especially Japanese whisky, no age statement versions have become increasingly common. Here is a damn good one. On the nose the aroma is sweet yet sharp. Make no mistake, this seems like a young whisky. Yet, there are traces of bonfire smoke and a fresh stream cascading over pebbles. It smells like camping deep in the forest. As for the taste, it's mouth-watering and there's a hint of berries followed by a spicy and smoky finish. An exceedingly balanced and well-made whisky.

Taketsuru Pure Malt 12 Years Old 85/100

Taketsuru Pure Malt is a blend of malts from the two distilleries Taketsuru created—the Yoichi Distillery in Hokkaido and the Miyagikyo Distillery in Sendai. Hence "Taketsuru." This one has wonderful aromas of figs, apricots, bamboo charcoal, mint, thyme, rosemary and wood. The palate has wonderful floral and grassy notes, with touches of moss and wet rocks. Taking a sip is like taking a step into a dense Japanese forest in early summer. It's refreshing and invigorating.

Taketsuru Pure Malt 17 Years Old 88/100

Nosing the glass, the aromas are deep and complex. There's the strong, sweet scent of American white oak casks. But waiting behind that you get smoke as well as aromas of watermelon, figs and molasses. The big body of this whisky brings alive the smoky and oaky flavors, and this 17-year-old has rustic, nostalgic qualities that evoke simpler days when large iron steam trains rhythmically made their way through dense Japanese forests.

Taketsuru Pure Malt 21 Years Old 88/100

The aromas aren't overpowered but refined. They linger above the glass. There's the smell of grass, orange peel and smoked fig. Those elegant aromas translate in a well-rounded and gentle palette. Wonderous stuff. It's a shame the Taketsuru line isn't nearly as popular as it should be in Japan.

Taketsuru Pure Malt Non-Chill Filtered 21 Years Old 86/100

One of the releases to celebrate Nikka's 80th anniversary, but in its "non-chill filtered" version. Bottled at 48 percent abv, it has lots of complex, terrific aromas. There are apricots, some light smoke and strawberries. The delivery is soft and crisp yet rich and creamy so that it turns around in the glass like a massive globe.

Taketsuru Pure Malt 25 Years Old 88/100

A limited edition bottling, this is one of the older Nikka Pure Malts. It's smoky and there are notes of bamboo charcoal and charred plum, with fruity sweetness that just seems to hang in the air. It's floral and very crisp. Taking a sip, it's soft, like newly fallen snow, but there's a warmth. Elegant and composed, there are notes of peeled apples, bookshelves and hay.

Yoichi Single Malt 12 Years Old

Yoichi Single Malt 15 Years Old

Taketsuru Pure Malt Sherry Wood Finish 68/100

Nikka's terrific Taketsuru blended malt with a sherry wood finish sounds like a great idea, but ... the sherry aromas are superficial, making the youth of this non-age statement whisky stand out even more. The delivery, however, is unexpectedly good and makes for a better sherried whisky experience than initially thought. But ... there's no lingering finish, no complexity and not much fun.

Yoichi Single Malt (No Age Statement) 87/100

Massive sales meant massive shortages. Starting in the fall of 2015, the Yoichi Distillery's single malt line-up was left with this non-aged expression. Considering how Nikka was caught flat-footed, making due with what stock it still had, the result is pretty good.

Scent-wise, there's Indian ink and the smell of an old brush, Japanese citron and rosewood, which follow through on arrival, as does metallic charcoal for a warm finish. All things considered, this is a daring expression

that's been whittled down to the bone. The result is a quietly refined whisky.

Yoichi Single Malt 10 Years Old 86/100

Nosing this whisky is like getting hit with a ton of bricks. The spicy cask notes are punchy while the strong smell of barley is intoxicating. But wait, what is this? The initial taste is a completely different experience. It's rather mellow. All that power does come roaring back in a long, salty finish.

Yoichi Single Malt 12 Years Old 83/100

Immediately, there are cask aromas, spice, salt and some slightly scorched barley. It's deep and rich. Taking a sip, the warm heat of alcohol is followed by toasted oats for a long finish.

Yoichi Single Malt 15 Years Old 89/100

This isn't a bouquet of white flowers but a field of them. The sweetness of honey is balanced with some light spice and faint apples. There are also

woody and nutty notes. Taste-wise, it's fruity and floral with growing, fresh spice for a long finish. Enchanting.

Yoichi Single Malt Peaty and Salty 12 Years Old 55/100

Okay, we've got a Yoichi single malt, which is already, at least for a Japanese whisky, rather smoky. But this is the smokier—rather, peatier—version with lots of salt. The label shows the Yoichi Distillery's pagoda towers, from which the peat smoke used to pour. These days Yoichi doesn't do its own maltings and, like many distilleries around the world, relies on outsourcing.

Putting your nose in the glass is like smelling *saketoba*, which is smoked salmon that has been dried into a jerky. And in the mouth? More salmon jerky but minus the chewing. It's so smoky you've got to wonder if fumes aren't wafting out of your nose after each taste. Bottled at 55 percent abv, this was available only at the Yoichi Distillery. It's a curious release, albeit not a very good one. The regular 12-year-old Yoichi is far superior. Heck, any regular Yoichi single malt is.

Yoichi 1987 Single Cask 22 Years Old 87/100

How is it? Quite good. First thing that you notice when nosing the glass is the delivery of sweet melon. Dry fruits and the smell of oak and sap. The delivery is refreshingly sweet, but as the flavor expands in the mouth, it changes into burning logs and sandalwood. But at the same time, unrefined, maybe too unrefined woody notes, take center stage. The finish is warm and this whisky suits a cold, peaceful day in winter.

HOMBO SHUZO
MARS WHISKY
SHINSHU DISTILLERY

The air is moist and the weather has unlocked a whole host of woodland smells, among them pine, fern and moss.

"When the sun's not out here, it's cold," says distillery manager Koki Takehira. It's fall now, but in winter when the distillery is covered in snow, Takehira adds, all the monkeys come down from the mountains and wander around the grounds. "There are more monkeys than distillery workers," he jokes. But no, the monkeys don't creep into the aging cellars and sneak sips of whisky.

Winter temperatures at Hombo Shuzo's Mars Whisky Shinshu Distillery average 30 °C (86 °F) but can drop to -15 °C (5 °F). Sitting at nearly 800 meters (2,625 feet) above sea level, this is the highest distillery in Japan. But the distillery wasn't always located here in Nagano Prefecture, an area traditionally known as Shinshu. Hombo Shuzo was born in Kagoshima, a region famous for *shochu* (see pages 15–16).

Above left The Shinshu Distillery on a rainy fall afternoon.
Left Shinshu Distillery manager Koki Takehira splits his time between making whisky and craft beer at the on-site brewery.
Below left Water from Japan's Southern Alps flows next to the Shinshu Distillery.
Above Kiichiro Iwai managed future Nikka founder Masataka Taketsuru while at Settsu Shuzo. In his later years, he joined Hombo Shuzo.
Right The first Mars Whisky pot stills sit next to the Shinshu Distillery's parking lot. If they look like Nikka's first pot stills at Yoichi, that's because their design was based on Taketsuru's notes from Scotland.

Founded in 1872 by Matsuzaemon Hombo, the company was originally involved in the textile business, as the first Western-style cotton mill had been built in Kagoshima several years earlier. But Japanese textiles had a hard time competing with cheaper imports, and in 1909 the company switched to making shochu. In 1949, Hombo Shuzo received a license to distill whisky. However, it wasn't until 1960 that it began distilling proper whisky at its previous location in Yamanashi Prefecture, which concentrated more on wine and less on whisky.

Mars Whisky moved to the newly built Shinshu Distillery in 1985. It's now Hombo's main distillery, but starting in late 2016 distillation began

at its Tsunuki Distillery in Kagoshima. Mars not only matures whisky at its Tsunuki and Shinshu plants but also at its sake brewery on Yakushima, a humid, moss-covered island south of Kyushu that inspired the location for the Studio Ghibli animated film *Princess Mononoke*.

Notes from the Father of Japanese Whisky

Even though this distillery has only been at its present location since the mid-1980s, it has a long, proud history and a direct link to one of the fathers of Japanese whisky.

"These are the original stills," says Takehira, pointing to a wash still and a spirit still next to the parking lot. "Kiichiro Iwai designed these stills based on notes Masataka Taketsuru made while in Scotland."

Prior to joining Hombo Shuzo, Iwai worked at Settsu Shuzo in Osaka, managing a brilliant young chemist by the name of Masataka Taketsuru, who reported his findings to Iwai upon return. This is why the Mars Shinshu pot stills are based on Taketsuru's

notes and how the maker has a direct connection to one of the fathers of Japanese whisky. Iwai joined Hombo Shuzo as a special advisor after its first proper whisky distillery was set up in 1960. When Iwai needed information about whisky stills, he pulled out Taketsuru's old notes for insights on how Scotland made malt whisky.

While Mars has a rich history, it's best to think of it as a relative newcomer or, rather, a returnee. "Whisky was distilled here until 1992," Mars Shinshu manager Koki Takehira says. Then, as sales slowed, the distillery was mothballed. Production stopped. "When we started up distillation again in 2011, there was only one employee who had made whisky." That employee, however, was at Hombo Shuzo's headquarters in Kagoshima, on the other side of the country.

Right Even though it's a separate company, the Minami Shishu Beer brewery is located on the same site.
Far right Before making and blending Mars whisky, Koki Takehira got his start pulling pints.

Beer Brewing Expertise

Takehira's first job at Shinshu wasn't making whisky. It wasn't even working at Mars. The distillery is also home to a small brewery for Minami Shinshu Beer, which was founded in 1996 when whisky production had stopped. Minami Shinshu Beer is not Japan's first craft beer brewery (that honor goes to Niigata's Echigo Beer) but it was certainly one of the first. Even though it's located on the distillery grounds, Minami Shinshu Beer is a separate company. Takehira got his start pulling pints part-time at the brewery's local tavern. Offering to create a computer database for the brewery led to him getting hired and working in the brewery, learning how to craft beer. "When Hombo Shuzo decided to restart whisky production, they approached me, saying that if I could brew beer, then I could probably figure out how to make whisky." Takehira was hired as the distillery manager but continues to do double duty working for the brewery. He wasn't the only one there new to whisky making.

When Hombo Shuzo announced that the Mars Distillery would be returning to whisky, it was big news within the

Japanese whisky business given the history the Mars brand has. "I was fortunate, because when it was announced this distillery was restarting, bigwigs at Suntory and Nikka visited and taught us various things," Takehira says. "Basically, they imparted how they made whisky and then it was up to us to decide whether or not we could use those techniques. If we could, we did, and if not, we didn't. Not every distillery in Japan is the same, and we are all trying to do what's best for the whisky we aim to make," he added.

"But getting back into the whisky making business wasn't so easy. Even though I had experience making beer, there were things that weren't clear to me when we restarted distillation." A metal staircase leads to a walkway next to where grain is milled and steeped and fermentation occurs. "This part of the process is like making beer," Takehira says. He knew how to do that much. But whisky? He was a novice. All Takehira had to go on was old documents which were basically workflows that listed things like distillation times, alcohol percentages and average temperatures during each step of the whisky-making process.

"We also had an internal company manual that listed each step for making whisky, but it was for people who already knew what they were doing. If you are starting at zero, you can't really follow along," Takehira says. "So, for example, it would just state 'milling,' but it wouldn't say what percentage needed to be husk, grist and flour." The percentage of each can impact the whisky's flavor, so to figure things out Takehira and the other distillers had to experiment. Takehira recalls how one time they milled a higher flour percentage and the mash tun got all clogged up. "It was difficult, and I was learning on the job," says Takehira. "Each of those mistakes taught me along the way."

As of 2017, the Shinshu distillery is using iron fermentation tanks dating from the 1960s. They're a throwback to another era in Japanese whisky production, before makers switched over to stainless steel or imported Douglas fir washbacks. Takehira, though, hopes to have new stainless steel tanks installed during future renovations. Other Japanese whisky makers use wooden washbacks to bring out lactic acid bacteria, which

add fruity aromas and flavors. The approach at Shinshu is different. "As much as possible we're trying not to bring out lactic acid bacteria because not doing so helps define the character of our whisky," Takehira says. "Mars Shinshu has a sweet and gentle malty character you just don't find in other Japanese whiskies."

When you have a beer brewer making whisky, you can bet a great deal of importance will be placed on the yeasts, and not just for alcohol yield but for flavor. Currently, the Mars Shinshu Distillery uses three different yeasts, which, by Japanese standards, is not many but is more than typically used in Scotland. One yeast is the original strain the distillery has used since 1985. Another is imported Scottish distiller's yeast, while the third one is ale yeast from the neighboring brewery. "For us," Takehira says, "we have lots of different beer yeasts to choose from that have different aromas, and from what we've

selected we have an ale yeast that we think best suits whisky."

At Mars there are two methods of adding yeast to the wort. For the imported distiller's yeast, which is a solid industrial yeast, it's added all at once. But for the in-house liquid yeast, it's added bit by bit, gradually increasing the amount and allowing the cells to multiply and become concentrated. In Japan, this type of yeasting is more common in sake production.

The Spirit of Shinshu

After four days the fermented beer is put in the wash still in the adjacent room for the first and second distillations. The two Japanese-made pot stills are near copies of the original stills sitting outside near the parking lot, with some modern updates, such as portholes on the still's neck to monitor distillation. On a placard near the wash still is a photo of Kiichiro Iwai together with a photo from Taketsuru's notebook (the original is on display at Nikka's Whisky Museum in Yoichi).

Iwai wasn't only brought in to make whisky but probably because he was less a whisky maker than a pro at producing alcohol, which he had done

at Settsu Shuzo and taught at university level. Now at Hombo Shuzo, they make single-distilled shochu but in the past it produced shochu using a continuous still. "That's why Hombo Shuzo asked him to come on board," Takehira says, also adding the fact that Iwai's daughter was the company president's wife probably factored into the elder Iwai taking a supervisory role at Hombo Shuzo. Once on board, the company looked into other areas to expand and whisky was one of them.

Taketsuru's original drawing was of a Hazelburn still. It served as the inspiration for the stills now at Yoichi as well as at Mars Shinshu, making it probably the single most influential drawing on the development of Japanese whisky. The still's shape helps define the character of the whisky. The angle of the lyne arm, which juts out from the neck, can decide if the spirit is light, with a heavy alcohol content but fewer flavors, or heavy, with a lighter alcohol content and robust flavors. It's the passageway for the vapor to pass, going into a condenser where the vapor is cooled into a liquid, and the angle decides what ratio alcohol, which is lighter than water, makes it through.

Left The still's lyne arm tapers off, resulting in a lighter distillate.
Above The distillery's small shrine is for the water god Mizugami (水神), also known as Suijin or Mizu no Kamisama. The deity's stone markers are found near rivers, rice paddies, canals, wells and even septic tanks.
Right The distillery has both a copper-colored "shell and tube" condenser (right, background) and a gray-colored worm tub (left, background).

At Mars Shinshu, the lyne arms are thin and narrow towards the end. Takehira points to the tube condenser into which the wash still's lyne arm feeds, saying, "The shell and tube condenser cool the distillate quickly and that results in a lighter whisky." He then points to the second still, the spirit still, with a lyne arm that feeds into a rotund tank. It's a worm tube. Inside, a copper coil slowly snakes its way through a tub of water, cooling the distillate in the process. "Cooling with warm tubs is much slower, producing a hardy spirit." Since Shinshu uses both methods of cooling, the result is a balanced whisky.

Stepping out of the still house, rain continues to fall. In the building next door is the beer brewery, and across the road is a small shrine less than a meter high. "That's for Mizugami, the deity of water," Takehira says. "Every morning before we start work, we come to this shrine and pray for safety and for good whisky." Water is a key part of Shintoism, which is centered around cleanliness and purity. Small shrines can be dedicated to a variety of *kami* or deities, which protect local areas from harm and misfortune.

The Future of Mars

Takehira opens the door to one of two on-site maturation warehouses. It's a rack-style warehouse, as is the other one. "We're going to be building a third one here but we need to be careful how we do it so that we don't impact the local environment." Enormous trees don't only surround the distillery but throughout the grounds there are huge, moss-covered boulders. The maturation warehouse is mostly filled with ex-bourbon barrels but there are also sherry butts, virgin American white oak casks and wine casks from Hombo Shuzo's winery.

"We have mizunara casks in the other maturation warehouse here at Shinshu," Takehira says. "We're looking at making whisky from local barely, and if we do I'd like us to make an all-Japanese whisky aged in mizunara. But using Japanese barley will definitely have an impact on the price because it's so expensive."

Mars imports its barley from Scotland and Germany. (In recent years, Scottish distilleries have also been having difficulty securing barley and many have also had to import a percentage from elsewhere in Europe.) Since his beer-brewing days, Takehira has been interested in domestic barley, which used to be the staple of both the whisky and beer businesses. The barley that Mars is testing is a two-row variety called Koharu from Iwate Prefecture that's used in beer. "There isn't much land in Japan so anything involving agriculture is expensive," he says. But it's more than that. There simply isn't the infrastructure there used to be—and the same goes for tariffs.

"Because of price controls, it was cheaper to use domestic barley in the past," Takehira says. Before World War II barley was a major crop in Japan, behind wheat and rice. Traditionally, it was grown to supplement rice but was regarded as an inferior grain. Due to a domestic barley crop surplus in the late 1950s, imports were suspended between 1960 and 1962. Decreased prices and a drop in local production meant that once imports were resumed there was an increase in foreign barley. "Over time, more and more malting stopped in Japan and because of this the country's malting techniques haven't improved in the way they have abroad." For Takehira, it's more than just a matter of getting domestic maltsters up and going. "Looking at this objectively, if we use Japanese barley it can't be enough to simply use the local crop," Takehira says. "The difference must be clear and noticeably good because if it's not and we're using expensive Japanese barley, then there's no point in doing it." Mars won't be doing the malting on-site but will farm it out to a Japanese beer maltster.

"Around the world whisky makers put great importance on the alcohol yield they get per ton of grain," says Takehira. "For me, that's still important, but if you can do something original, then that's worth the extra cost, even if the yield is lower."

Below Casks stacked high at the Shinshu Distillery's racked warehouse.
Bottom A 458-liter (121-gallon) cask reading "Shinsyu Distillery." The Japanese character しゅ can be romanized as either "shu" or "syu," with the "shu" romanization being more common.

Creating a New Japanese Whisky Culture

The sound of rain pattering on the roof echoes throughout the maturation cellar. "What I really want to do is create a culture," Takehira says. "When the Japanese whisky boom is over, if you are producing great whiskies you not only create a new culture but you become entrenched in it. That's what I want to do." Scotland has the Scotch Whisky Association, he says, set up to protect and promote the country's industry but Japan has nothing like it.

"We have the Japan Spirits and Liqueurs Makers Association but it's not only for whisky distillers," he says, adding that it also includes vodka, gin, brandy and plum liqueur makers, among others. "We need an association that's only for Japanese whisky." He believes that such an association could help standardize practices within the industry and help distilleries share information, but also help ensure quality. "Right now, people outside Japan have a very good impression of Japanese whisky, so we need to make sure that does not change." If all Japanese whisky doesn't play by the same rules, it might.

"Personally, I think Japanese whisky needs to be distilled entirely in Japan," says Takehira as he opens the door to the aging warehouse, watching the rain fall. "I didn't think too deeply about this in 2011, but in 2012, when I started buying bulk Scotch grain whisky for our blends, the Scotch Whisky Association asked me what I was going to use it for," he

The Tsunuki Distillery

"At our new whisky Tsunuki Distillery in Kagoshima, where Hombo Shuzo is based, we are distilling a much heavier whisky," says Takehira. Both stills are squat and onion-shaped, with lyne arms that angle down, collecting the vapor for the wash and spirit stills in worm tubs where the distillates will slowly cool. The aim is a robust, full-bodied spirit.

The distillery might be "new" but this isn't the first time Mars has made whisky in Kagoshima. From the early 1950s to 1985, it made whisky before concentrating on shochu, the region's most famous drink. The Tsunuki Distillery has the same capacity as the Shinshu outfit and is now the southernmost whisky distillery in the country. Aging is done on-site in dunnage warehouses. Mars has also been maturing whisky at its sake brewery on Yakushima, a small island in Kagoshima Prefecture. All of this gives Mars more options to make a variety of different whiskies in-house.

"In Scotland, whisky makers usually have only one distillery, but in Japan one maker might have two distilleries that are vastly different in character in order to produce a wide range of malts as well as to create suitable blends between the locations." Kagoshima is the alpha to Shinshu's beta. What inspired the big, flavorful spirit was Sakurajima, the active volcano in Kagoshima. The aim is a spirit that is just as fiery as the volcano.

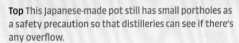

Top This Japanese-made pot still has small portholes as a safety precaution so that distilleries can see if there's any overflow.
Above Burgundy doors at the Tsunuki Distillery's stone-faced warehouse.

Above A distillery worker fills a cask with new-made distillate.
Right In the foreground is a hybrid still used to distill gin. Mars has joined Number One Drinks and Nikka in producing quality Japanese gin.

Far right A distillery worker checks the new-made spirit in the spirit safe.

Right A close-up of the Tsunuki Distillery uniform.

Below The Tsunuki Distillery has a large French-made continuous still that's no longer in use. It's housed in a black building with a red roof that marks the distillery from afar.

Above Heating coils inside a Tsunuki pot still.

Above right A distiller pours new make spirit into a beaker to check the quality.

Right Temperature is one way distillers can find the "heart" of the distillation run.

says. "I realized that Scotch whisky makers noticed that smaller Japanese distilleries like this, which don't have grain whisky distilleries, are using their whisky in blends and that there's even cause for concern."

The worry was that small Japanese whisky companies were trying to pass off their whiskies blended with Scotch grain whisky as Japanese. Now there are some new whisky brands that are buying Scotch and aging it in Japan because they don't have distillation equipment. But as Whyte & Mackay master blender Richard Patterson recounted in his memoirs, during the 1970s Japan's biggest distillers were buying bulk Scotch malt whisky "to enhance their own blends." The practice became controversial enough in Scotland that *Reuters* reported in October 1977 how concerned whisky industry folks held a protest in Glasgow demanding a reduction in bulk exportation to Japan and saying they thought the country was a "real threat" to Scotch. Even though Japanese whisky exports were miniscule at the time, a Scotch Whisky Association spokesperson explained, "I think it would be totally foolish to underrate the commercial and selling skills of the Japanese."

The practice of importing bulk Scotch into Japan continues, and

in recent years it has been on the upswing. According to a 2016 US agricultural trade report on the Japanese whisky market, the country's makers increased their import of bulk whisky to create blends to overcome shortages. "This is partly responsible for the jump in whisky volumes over the last two years," the report added.

Mars Whisky, now focusing more on its malts, is using some Japanese grain whisky in its blends. Tor Takehira, it's been a realization that his industry needs standards and guidelines to define what exactly Japanese whisky is, especially because around the world there is so much goodwill towards Japanese whisky, with customers automatically assuming that whatever comes

Above left Built in 1933, the former home of Hombo Shuzo's second president, Tsuneyoshi Hombo, sits across from the Tsunuki Distillery. The family's crest depicts a paper mulberry leaf, which is associated with Shinto shrine offerings and the white folded strips on Shinto garlands.
Above The home has been converted into a cafe, gift shop and bar.
Below Whisky aging at Tsunuki can be blended with Shinshu aged spirit for new Mars whiskies.

out of Japan is good. "It hit me that day that some sort of reckoning could come early, so we do need an association for standardization."

For now Takehira opens his umbrella and holds out his hand to check for rain. "I bet it'll be sunny this afternoon," he says before heading out.

TASTING NOTES FOR 13 HOMBO SHUZO WHISKIES

By Yuji Kawasaki

There is a notion that Japanese whisky is created by design. That's not true of every maker, and it's certainly not true of Mars, which tends to bring a certain rough and even intuitive quality to its malt whiskies. The Mars Shinshu single malts and blends have wonderful old wood flavors accented with leafy green notes. Shinshu already packs a punch, so it'll be exciting to see what the Tsunuki Distillery brings.

Iwai Tradition Wine Cask Finish
85/100

This blend was finished in a wine cask for a year. There's a fragrant top note, the scent of roses and the warm aroma of a botanical garden. Under that there is a sweet, salty aroma. All of this leads to lush, soft flavors and warming spice.

Komagatake The Revival 2011
56/100

The Hombo Mars Distillery's first release since it resumed distilling whisky in 2011 after ceasing production in 1992. This then is "The Revival." The word "Komagatake" refers to Mount Komagatake, the base of which sits the Mars Distillery.

Aged for three years in American oak, it's a young, lightly peated whisky, limited to 6,000 bottles. The first thing that hits you on the nose is the alcohol! Mars bottled this single malt at 58 percent. You do get the delicious freshness of taking a walk through a moss-covered forest in June, during Japan's rainy season. The biggest impression is how invigorating this whisky is. But more maturation time would benefit this very young spirit, making it as good as it should've been, especially for its price tag.

Komagatake Pure Malt Whisky 10 Years Old 78/100

There's the smell of dried barley, with a fluffy pillow-like softness to the aroma. With the first sip's arrival, what comes to mind is a field of grass in summertime taking hold and the wind gently blowing. Refreshing and evocative.

Komagatake Bartenders Choice Chateau Mars Wine Cask Finish
83/100

The first aromas that leap out are strawberry and sour fruits like kiwi but in the background there are warm, gentle notes of *saketoba* or dried salmon jerky. This whisky is surprisingly smooth in ways you might not expect, with some hints of smoke.

Iwai Tradition Wine Cask Finish

Komagatake The Revival 2011

Komagatake Pure Malt Whisky 10 Years Old

The Lucky Cat "Sun" Port and Madeira Cask Finish

Twin Alps

Komagatake Single Cask 1988 25 Years Old **89/100**

From 1992 to 2011 Mars didn't distill. During that time, this whisky was waiting. Bottled in 2013, this single cask shows what Mars whiskies can do if they're given enough time. It's a shame that Mars was only able to release 468 bottles of this stuff.

The result is a big, spicy, sherried whisky, underscored with notes of unripe fruit and burnt wood. It's smooth, but then those spices kick in. That's when the unripe fruit follows, soothing the experience. In Japan, throughout the summer, there are huge fireworks displays, with thousands of beautiful explosions fired over rivers. But when they end, the rivers and skies are once again placid. Just like this whisky.

The Lucky Cat "Sun" Port and Madeira Cask Finish **86/100**

The label is, well, different. It features a photo of a feline, which is one way of appealing to both fans of whisky and cats. Inside the bottle is a blended spirit aged in oak and then finished in port and madeira casks. Gently nosing the glass there's poppy flowers, fresh soil and even red crayon. Taking a sip, the mouthfeel is soft and smooth, like a cat spread out on a carpet, stretching and yawning. The result is one relaxing dram.

Twin Alps **78/100**

Priced at 1,922 yen (US$17), this is a terrific budget blend. What makes it so good? It's a rather simple yet noble whisky. There's a fair amount of oak (and alcohol) on the nose. If you've ever wondered what an old Japanese schoolhouse smells like, try this. Holding it in your mouth, you start to get sweet, soft fruits like strawberries, followed by more wood and then spiciness on the palette. Twin Alps punches well above its price range.

Mars Maltage 3 Plus 25 Pure Malt Whisky 28 Years Old **87/100**

This World Whisky Award-winning blended malt whisky is actually a 28-year-old. "3 Plus 25" means that the whiskies in this blend were aged for three years in Kagoshima and 25 years in Nagano Prefecture where the Shinshu Distillery is located.

Nosing the glass, there's a plump sweetness. Underneath that, spices and sharp wood aromas appear on the alcohol, along with smoked freshwater fish. On arrival, it's invigoratingly sweet, like summer fruit. As the 46 percent alcohol makes this whisky hot, that's when it's possible to slowly experience the delicious malty flavors. The finish, though, is where the sweetness once again returns.

The Malt of Kagoshima H. Bolina **93/100**

Here's a super rare one. Limited to 111 bottles, this was originally distilled in 1984 at Mars Whisky's Kagoshima

Mars Maltage 3 Plus 25 Pure Malt Whisky
28 Years Old

Komagatake Single Malt Nature of
Shinshu Rindo

Distillery, which was brought back online in 2016 for whisky production. The "H. Bolina" refers to Hypolimnas bolina, aka the blue moon butterfly for its dark blue and lunar-like markings.

The first note is European oak. This whisky has been aged for 25 years in sherry casks and there is a slight sweetness. The nose on this, though, isn't overpowering but flutters about. In the background there are coffee and fresh green leaves.

Tastewise, this is like brand-new calf skin leather gloves. Some mineraliness. It's a lucid whisky, though, like a mid-winter sky or that moment the ocean just comes into view and is glittering in the light. Any which way you look at it, there is only one conclusion. This malt makes for one beautiful dram.

Komagatake Single Cask 1988 #566 90/100

You don't need to stick your nose in this whisky, the aromas just rise right out of the glass. Lots of smoke and burnt wood, reminiscent of an old fireplace. But crispy, leafy menthol balances out the aroma. The arrival is spicy yet develops into a gentle, smooth sweetness that envelopes the tongue and seems to stop time. The result is a mystical experience that's only possible with whisky.

Komagatake Single Cask 1988 #557 89/100

Spring. There are fragrant woodland flowers, with a nearby clear brook and big trees. The spices are balanced and the palate is harmonious. It's pictur-esque, and spending time with this whisky is akin to gazing at a delightful landscape.

Komagatake Single Malt Nature of Shinshu Rindo 85/100

Satisfying, encompassing aromas on this one. The top note is dignified sweetness, under which there is a settled and slight smokiness. "Rindo" refers to Japanese gentian, the dark blue flowers that bloom in summer and fall and the representative flower of Nagano Prefecture where the Shinshu Distillery is located.

Bottled at 52 percent alcohol, this single malt is composed of whisky distilled in 2012 and older Mars whiskies that are over 20 years old. Taking a sip, that sweetness really comes alive with just the right amount of spice, followed by a refreshing finish that's reminiscent of a breeze over Nagano's grassy fields and one that's often found in Mars' Komagatake malts. A composed, beautiful whisky.

Shinshu Mars Whisky Phoenix and the Sun 2012–2015 75/100

Sticking your nose in this whisky is like getting punched in the gut. It's rough, like just whittled wood. The alcohol is so sharp and this whisky is so young, you're left wondering, is this drinkable? Taking a small sip, damn it's spicy. But, wait, there is a softness. There is a barely manageable consistency about the experience, and even though this isn't quite matured, it is savory, tipped off with some freshly ground black pepper.

A limited edition bottling for a whisky talk event in Fukuoka, this three-year-old whisky was distilled in 2012, aged in American white oak and then bottled in 2015. Three years of maturation might be too short, but if you are spending a frigid winter by the Sea of Japan, a bottle of this would come in handy.

KIRIN FUJI GOTEMBA DISTILLERY

On a clear day you can see Mt Fuji. Whether you stand in a grassy field or in front of a 7-Eleven off the highway, the view is spectacular. For the Japanese, this isn't just a mountain. Shinto shrines, with their devotion to nature, dot its peaks, and its summit is the premier place for climbers to see the first sunrise of the year. No wonder the mountain has touched deep within the national psyche and has come to represent the country itself. That's why few backdrops in the world are as dramatic as this for making whisky.

Kirin only has one whisky distillery in the world. It sure did a nice job of selecting this locale in the town of Gotemba. But it didn't act alone. Previously, this was an international collaborative effort between the home-grown Kirin, North America's Joseph E. Seagram & Sons and the United Kingdom's Chivas Brothers. The then-named Kirin Seagrams was established in 1972 and began distilling a year later. The concept was to make whiskies that would appeal to Japanese customers who might have been more inclined to import Scottish or Canadian blends. The result was a string of approachable whiskies.

In 2002, Kirin took 100 percent sole control of the whisky operation, renaming itself the Kirin Distillery. While other Japanese distilleries release older, very expensive single malts, the

Kirin Distillery is unique in that besides the aged grain whiskies it puts out for hundreds of dollars, it also continues to produce its affordable supermarket blends, including the non-chilled filtered Fuji Sanroku.

But what makes Kirin truly special is how such a big distillery produces such an enormous variety

Top Whether you're on the highway, riding the bullet train or at the Kirin Distillery, Mt Fuji is hard to miss.
Center The red structure with Kirin Distillery's crest is a cleverly disguised grain silo. The buildings to the left house the fermentation and distillation rooms.
Above The author takes notes as master distiller Osamu Igura discusses the merits of grain whisky.

of vastly different types of whiskies all on-site and in close proximity, ranging from an array of grain whiskies to Scottish-style lightly peated single malts. The malt whisky pot stills are in the room adjacent to the grain spirit multi-column stills, while the kettle and the doubler are just downstairs. Moreover, unlike many famous Japanese distilleries, which now bottle their whiskies off-site, Kirin still does it all at the distillery.

Whisky from Mount Fuji

Back in the early 1970s, after several years of searching, this spot was picked for two main reasons. Located at 619 meters (2,030 feet) above sea level, the

average annual temperature is 13 °C (55 °F), which is consistently cooler and less humid than elsewhere on Japan's main island and thus closer to Scotland's climate.

The other big reason is the water source. Mt Fuji isn't only a dramatic backdrop for whisky making, it also provides Kirin's water. According to the distillery, the moment ice melts, it takes around 50 years to filter through sediment left by volcanic eruptions over the past 10,000 years. Kirin is so pleased with this source that it bottles and sells the Mt Fuji water it uses to make whisky.

The Heart of Kirin

Decked out in an immaculate work uniform, master distiller Osamu Igura is tall, with sharp features. Behind him stands one of three copper brown lantern-shaped pot stills. There used to be four in use, but in 2016 one of the spirit stills was put out to pasture as an interactive part of the distillery tour, allowing visitors to get a close-up look. As of 2017, Kirin was only using two of its pot stills to make whisky, with the extra wash still in a holding position. Each pot still's lyne arm angles up, Kirin says, producing a clean, estery

spirit leading into the condensers. Kirin doesn't just use the heart of the distillate but the "heart of the heart," which is an even narrower section of the distillate's smoothest part.

"Grain whisky, however, is our specialty, because we have that expertise," Igura says. Kirin makes three types of grain spirit—light, medium and heavy. American corn, which produces an unmistakable sweet profile, dominates the mash bill, or the percentage of each grain used. However, rye can also be added

Top With more Japanese distilleries charging a fee, the Kirin Distillery has, at the time of writing, one of the increasingly rare free distillery tours.

Above As of spring 2016, the Kirin Distillery was doing maturation tests in Oloroso sherry butts and Japanese oak casks. The larger casks will not fit in Kirin's racked warehouses.

Left Besides distilling malt whisky in pot stills, the Kirin Distillery also makes three types of grain whiskies using three different set-ups. This diversity is a rarity in the whisky world. In recent years, Kirin has been releasing a wider array of whiskies, taking advantage of that uniqueness.

to impart its own spicy characteristics. Malted Scottish barley is also added to produce necessary enzymes to break down starches and create simple sugars. Yeast from Kirin's vast collection is then added to the mash and fermented for three days.

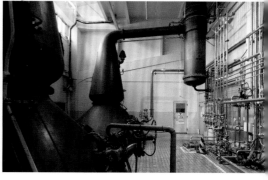

"We did try making whisky from rice," says Igura. Rice might be a grain but distilling it sounds a lot closer to *shochu*, which can be made from rice, than whisky (for more on shochu, see pages 15–16). So, how did Kirin's experiment go? "Not well," Igura says with a smile.

A Collection of Towering Stills

Past the control room and through a door into another hall, Igura points to five towers of various heights. The set-up is a multi-column still, with the wash cycled through the multiple stills, producing raw grain whisky. "It makes a light spirit," Igura says. Light doesn't mean weak. The raw distillate it produces measures between 90 and 94 percent alcohol. It's a clean spirit with fewer aromas and flavors than found in the malt whisky.

Still early spring, the air is cool in the Column Still Room. "It gets to 50 °C [122 °F] in this room in summer," Igura says. "We have to open all the windows. It's great, though, in winter."

During the 1980s, when Kirin was running at full capacity, Igura says they did malt and grain distilling at the same time. Now, Kirin only distills one at a time, on alternate days. Not all the spirit distilled here goes into whisky. The column stills also make the alcohol for Kirin's popular ready-to-drink alcoholic beverages, including canned *chu-hai* (shochu highballs).

"On a monthly basis, there's a test for us, the distillers," Igura says. Two Kirin blends are poured for the distillers, who must tell them apart in a blind taste test. Correctly identifying them means they've passed. Failing can mean one's distilling days are numbered.

As with many huge distilleries, automation and computers help produce a steady flow of high-quality spirit, but it's distillers like Igura who ensure it's up to scratch. "Every eight hours we check the spirit by nosing it to ensure its consistent quality," Igura says, guesturing to the spirit safe. It's not a box-type spirit safe in the classical sense but more a stainless table with curved metallic tubes.

Igura rests his hands on the metal table in front of the spirit safe, saying, "We distillers made this table by hand and fix things here when we have to." He seems as proud of the metallic table as of his whisky. Both are, in different ways, expressions of love for the craft of distilling.

Above The silver tank on the right is the doubler, which enables Kirin to make a heavy, bourbon-like grain spirit.
Right The towering multi-column stills produce a light grain spirit at 94 percent abv.

Where Bourbon Meets Japanese Whisky

An elevator leads downs to the first floor. There's a kettle-style still that works with the multi-column still's rectifier and beer column to produce a medium-type grain spirit. Another unusual piece of equipment, at least for Japan, is right next to the kettle.

"This is the only distillery in Japan that has a doubler," Igura says, pointing. Doublers, or "thumpers," are used in bourbon distillation in the United States. Working with the multi-column still's beer column, the doubler is a massive, nondescript metal tank that does the second distillation and produces a heavy grain spirit. "This makes a spirit that is very close to bourbon," Igura says. Of course, it cannot be called bourbon, for the same reasons that not all sparkling white wine is called champagne.

Unlike in Scotland, where distilleries are using rather uniform yeasts, American distillers put huge emphasis on their unique strands, using yeast to bring out certain characteristics during fermentation which carry over into the finished whisky. Likewise, Kirin, with its expertise in beer brewing, can tweak the flavors with any of its hundreds of different yeast strands.

But it's not only the equipment that is reminiscent of bourbon. Kirin owns the Four Roses Distillery in Kentucky where it sent current master blender Jota Tanaka to work under master distiller Jim Rutledge. They co-developed Four Roses' excellent Single Barrel and Small Batch bourbons. Tanaka brings that deep knowledge of bourbon and grain whisky to his blends, while Four Roses sends its bourbon barrels to Japan, where they age Kirin's distilled spirit. The result is much more than simply a Japanese take on American whiskey.

The Top of Kirin's Maturation Warehouse

Past sliced barrels that have been turned into planters and filled with bonsai trees, a winding road leads to the distillery's warehouses. Over half of the grounds are covered in trees. *Fujizakura*, a regional type of cherry blossom, giving bursts of pink to the surrounding woods, which in summer are filled with fireflies.

At the end of the road is an 10-story aging warehouse, one of five maturation sites at Gotemba, in which anywhere from 35,000 to 50,000 whisky casks sleep. Warehouse worker Masaru Takasugi pulls open the massive doors. Stepping inside, the aroma of pancakes covered with maple syrup starts out subtly and gets more intense. It's quiet, solemn and cool, and combined with the way the metal racks ascend into the sky, the warehouse feels like a cathedral. "It's usually much noisier in here when we're loading and unloading barrels," Takasugi says, "and in summer the upper racks feel like a sauna. We're covered in sweat."

American white oak barrels, with the majority sourced from Kirin-owned Four Roses Distillery, rule the warehouse. There is a good reason for this. The warehouse racks are designed to only hold 180-liter (40-gallon) barrels since these are smaller than

sherry butts, which are up to 500 liters (132 gallons) and hogsheads, which are between 225 and 250 liters (60 and 66 gallons). But because of their smaller size, casks at Kirin ensure plenty of interaction between the spirit and the American oak during maturation.

Kirin is experimenting and testing with other kinds of casks. Later, in the dumping area, where all the whisky is poured out of the barrels, Kirin Distillery spokesperson Kazuki Nakagawa points to an Oloroso sherry cask filled with Kirin whisky. "We've also been doing trials with *mizunara* casks," Nakagawa adds, "to see how they flavor our whisky."

Back in the warehouse, Takasugi climbs into a small cart and presses a green button. An alarm sounds, lights flash and the cart moves slowly like an elevator

into the warehouse's upper reaches. "We put the whiskies wherever we can," Takasugi says, pointing to open spaces that are passed along the way. "We don't really have certain whiskies that go in certain places."

The cart stops at the highest level, 10 stories up. "This is the first time I've been up here," says Nakagawa, who seems to have slight vertigo. The view is incredible and the scent of honeyed oak and sweet syrup is delicious as the alcohol vapors tickle the throat while the whisky continues to quietly sleep.

Above The top rack of this Fuji Gotemba maturation warehouse gets hot in summer. These casks are bourbon barrels, which Kirin acquires from its subsidiary, Four Roses Bourbon. Cooperage company Showa Yotal Konki, which split off from former cooperage Showa Yotal, handles Kirin's on-site cask management.
Left The racks at Kirin's maturation warehouses are designed to hold 180-liter (40 gallon) barrels.

Bottled Up

The clank of glass and the squeal of machines echo throughout the bottling line. Some 150 bottles pass through the line in a single minute, while up on the wall an electronic board keeps track of the progress and daily targets.

A woman watches the bottles pass under fluorescent lights to check the clarity, occasionally touching the caps to make sure they're closed and pulling out the bottles that aren't up to snuff. The bottles then wind through a labeling machine and there's the sound of a pistol as labels are affixed on the spinning bottles. Checking the bottles is tiring on the eyes, hence breaks every 50 minutes.

The Fuji Sanroku blend's labels proudly read "non-chill filtered." Kirin does add caramel coloring to ensure a consist hue but stopped selling chilled-filtered Sanroku in spring 2016. Chill filtering happens before bottling and removes any residue and small particles. It's to prevent natural haziness, known as "Scotch mist," that forms in the whisky when water or ice is added. Malt whisky is typically brought down to anywhere between 0 degrees Celsius to minus four and then filtered. Does chill filtering really impact the flavor or mouth feel of whisky? That's still uncertain, but many distillers and

Above A bottling plant worker checks the whisky's color.
Left After the bottles are labeled, they are once again checked for imperfections.
Below Kirin's chu-hai or "shochu highball" beverages are also churned out at the Kirin Distillery. In the foreground, Kirin Whisky Fuji Sanroku is bottled and packed, while on the left Kirin's Hyoketsu brand chu-hai is canned and packed into boxes.

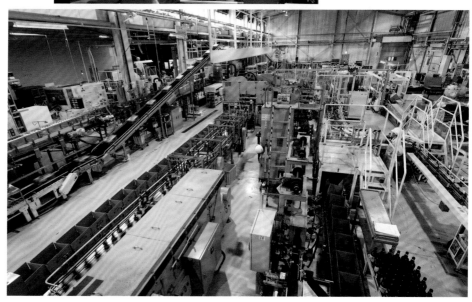

whisky lovers swear by non-chill filtered whiskies.

"We had the idea a few years ago," says Igura. "We ran some tests and decided to release this blend as non-chill filtered." Fuji Sanroku is reasonably priced, and for whiskies in this range non-chilled filtered is rare, especially in Japan. It's something you see on much more expensive premium whiskies, not on a budget-priced supermarket whisky.

In the bottling plant, off in the back corner, there is the dull clank of cans.

Chu-hai, which is often flavored with fruit juice such as lemon or lime, is getting canned and boxed for shipment. These ready-to-drink beverages are a Japanese favorite and have been since the 1980s. Whether it's a weekend picnic or at home watching TV, canned chu-hai is everywhere. For years, Kirin didn't show this canning line to those outside the company. "Probably among distillers here," says Nagakawa, "ready-to-drink chu-hai used to be seen as a rival to whisky." Those canned drinks might pay the bills, but for

those at the stills and in the blending lab, Kirin Distillery sees itself as first and foremost a whisky distillery.

"The whisky business has its ups and downs like waves," Igura says gesturing. He recalls how the late 1980s led to a very bad stretch and how things slowed down significantly in the years that followed. Production now has increased dramatically, while Kirin Distillery redid its visitors' center and distillery tour, ready to greet Japanese whisky fans. "We're really proud of our whisky," Igura says. They should be.

TASTING NOTES FOR 8 KIRIN WHISKIES

By Yuji Kawasaki

The Kirin Distillery's production methods are unique among Japanese makers and result in light, smooth whiskies that, at their best, are honed and polished. In many ways they're similar to Japanese *dashi*, or soup broth, and filled with savory flavors. Typically in Kirin's whiskies, the sweetness of corn doesn't feel cloying.

Fuji Gotemba Distillery Blended Whisky Kunpu 2015 89/100
"Kunpu" means "summer breeze," and Kirin's Kunpu blends show off some of the best the distillery has to offer. First up, subtle aromas. Flower, honey and softy woody smoke. Then come the vanilla and rose, which just blossom upon arrival. This is a beautiful and noble whisky.

Fuji Gotemba Distillery Blended Whisky Kunpu 2016 86/100
Another excellent Kunpu release from Kirin. Flowing raspberries for a slightly fancy nose. It's light, with a good aftertaste, conveying delicate charred cask notes.

Fuji Gotemba Distillery Single Grain Whisky 25 Years Old 92/100
Right off, you notice the softness. The feeling is like being in a forest bathed in gentle light. The traces of sweet muscat are like a sauce you'd find drizzled over a dessert. It has

Kirin Whisky Single Malt 18 Years Old

Kirin Distillery Pure Malt Whisky 20th Anniversary

Kirin Whisky Fuji Sanroku

Kirin Whisky Oak Master

wonderful chocolate notes, too.

The taste of this liquor constantly changes. It's fresh, then slightly withered, and the experience is like concentrating on sand slowly falling in an hourglass. The smoothness absorbs you right up, and the finish is exceedingly long, giving this whisky so much character.

Fuji Gotemba Distillery Single Malt Whisky Small Batch 17 Years Old 82/100

Eye-opening menthol, followed by refreshing sweetness. On delivery, the way the sharpness expands is unexpected, but this intensity is refined with biscuits dipped in muscat grapes. The whole experience becomes inherently delicate.

Kirin Distillery Pure Malt Whisky 20th Anniversary 68/100

Imagine a gentle rug on a grassy field that you stretch out and sleep on. You can feel the breeze as you look at the clouds in the sky. That's pretty much this anniversary whisky. It's a rather breezy affair, but what stands out is just how soft it is. Sadly, there's not much more going on beyond that.

Kirin Whisky Fuji Sanroku 72/100

Not only is this budget-priced whisky non-chilled filtered, it's bottled at 50 percent alcohol, making it excellent value. This one has corn and bourbon written all over it. The corn aromas are clear and just spread on arrival, getting increasingly hot. The mouthfeel is soft, as though this is a Japanese bourbon. This makes sense because among Japanese whiskies it's rare to see flavors and aromas this close to bourbon.

Kirin Whisky Oak Master 56/100

On the nose, there's mature grain mixed with oak aromas. It's soft, like the way wood bends. Gradually, various casks in this blend put in appearances, with grain being the base here and the wood serving as fragrance. There is, however, no complexity.

Kirin Whisky Single Malt Fuji Sanroku 18 Years Old 85/100

While there are floral notes, they're closer to charred, dried flowers. Even at 43 percent alcohol, this is a hot, peppery whisky, reminiscent of burning leaves during fall. There is a skin-tingling lucidity, like a bright morning in the mountains, as well as a fresh woodiness. Just as the warm finish begins, those floral notes bloom once again, if only for an instant.

VENTURE WHISKY
CHICHIBU DISTILLERY

M orning mist rolls through the mountains. The air smells of blossoms and the grass is covered with dew. It's early and a rooster crows at a nearby farm. This is Chichibu, Saitama Prefecture. The region is long famous for silk and sake, but these days it's known for something else—whisky.

"Chichibu" in Japanese is 秩父, with the first character 秩 referring to "order" and the second character 父 meaning "father." There couldn't be a more fitting name for this distillery.

A Dynasty of Sake Brewers
Founder Ichiro Akuto didn't only select this locale because it looked like a great place to distill. "I grew up here

in Chichibu," says Akuto, decked out in a lab coat, going through handwritten notebooks in his blender's lab, located in what appears like a typical suburban Japanese house. Inside, though, it's anything but. Large glass windows separate the hallway from the blending lab, a completely white room with shelves filled with whisky samples. When Akuto blends, however, it looks more like cooking, with him adding a dash of this and pouring a splash of that, jotting notes along the way. "I go back later and measure it out exactly once I've created something I'm happy with."

Akuto, in his early fifties, founded the distillery in 2004. This wasn't a family first. "I'm the 21st generation to make liquor," he says. The Akutos started brewing sake in 1625, and in 1941 Akuto's grandfather founded drinks maker Toa Shuzo in the nearby city of Hanyu. The distillery originally

Above Unfortunately, the Chichibu Distillery is not open to the general public. The distillery is so small, a continous stream of tours would make whisky production difficult, if not impossible.
Left Leaves change color at Chichibu during fall. The wash still in the foreground is from the Hanyu Distillery.

Above Venture Whisky's Ichiro Akuto explains his approach to blending.

Top right Ichiro's Malt and Grain ready for shipping.

Center right Since the Chichibu Distillery only has one labeling machine, it means that half of the bottle line must affix labels the old-fashioned way—by hand.

Below right Venture Whisky doesn't add caramel dye to its whiskies. The color is the natural result of wood maturation.

made *goseishu*, or "synthetic sake," which was diluted sake with distilled alcohol because rice was a wartime scarcity. The American military occupation provided new customers, thirsty GIs, and in 1946 Toa Shuzo got a whisky distilling license. "I don't think they made real whisky, though," Akuto says. "Although I've never had what they distilled." In the decades that followed, the company also imported whisky from Scotland for blending. Thinking it would be cheaper to distill malt spirit in Japan, his father set up proper pot stills in 1983 at what's now known as the Hanyu Distillery. Good whisky but bad luck followed.

The next year marked the first decline in the country's whisky consumption. The year after that, 1985, brought the Plaza Accord agreement, which was designed to depreciate the strong US dollar. In the early 1980s, the US dollar was rapidly appreciating against the yen, giving Japanese companies a huge edge. The Plaza Accord worked and the value of the greenback was cut in half. The yen, however, spiked the following year, making it more expensive for Toa Shuzo to distill in Japan than to import Scotch spirit. Changing Japanese liquor tax laws, Akuto explains, later that decade didn't help either.

The Hanyu Distillery was also going up against the country's drinking culture. "At that period in Japan, *mizuwari*, whisky with water, was most popular and Hanyu whisky was ahead of its time," he says. Japan still wasn't quite ready.

Father and Son

Akuto didn't start his whisky-making career at his family's distillery. "After I finished university I got a job at Suntory," he recalls. "I dreamt of making whisky at Yamazaki but they put me in the marketing section. That's how it often works in large Japanese companies. You don't have a choice and are assigned to certain areas." Akuto showed a knack for marketing, adding, "I was good at sales and liked it okay." But the feeling that he really wanted to make whisky lingered.

"Just as I wondered if I was really meant for this, my dad called me, saying his business wasn't doing well and asked me to come back home and help." For Akuto, this wasn't just a way to help the family but possibly to start his own whisky-making career. "In Japan, you must be brave to quit working for a big company," Akuto says. Suntory is a major player and working for an entity like that offers security. "But what I really wanted to do won out." Akuto was coming home. "Sure, I had worked in the whisky business in Japan before but I didn't learn the joy of making whisky until I entered my father's company."

While at Toa Shuzo, then the family business, Akuto still primarily handled sales but had learned how whisky was crafted, working in the distillery when he could. "I didn't get any advice on

Left Akuto noses spirit to tell the stillman when to make the cut.
Below A *kamidana* hangs on the distillery wall near the pot stills. On each white vase, it reads, "Before god." The sacred *sakaki* (*Cleyera japonica*) branches are traditional offerings at Shinto shrines. On the right in the back is an *ofuda*, which is a Shinto tailsman. This one is from sake shrine Matsunoo Taisha in Kyoto.

making whisky from my father per se," Akuto says. "Most of what I learned was from those on the distillery floor." However, the company's bottom line wasn't getting any better and the Japanese whisky business was bottoming out. Prospects were so grim that Toa Shuzo ended up being sold and the company's new owner wasn't interested in making whisky. In May 2004, the company was bought out. "We didn't see eye to eye, so I left," he says. That September Akuto established Venture Whisky.

The new owner didn't even seem interested in the casks of Hanyu whisky. Since Akuto didn't yet have a license to store alcohol, Sasanokawa Shuzo, a sake and shochu maker dating from 1765, purchased the remaining Hanyu stock in 2004, rescuing those casks of malt whisky for him. "I had wondered what people who really loved and knew whisky thought of my dad's whisky, so the following spring I took a bottle to a famous whisky bar in Tokyo," Akuto says. The bartender at the well-known Helmsdale, which is filled with classic and rare whiskies, was quite impressed and offered to make introductions to other bars.

"Until then I hadn't heard anyone praise my father's whisky," he says. "I was so happy." Akuto, however, didn't stop there. While trying to set up his own distillery, he went from Tokyo bar to Tokyo bar, night after night for a year, trying to interest them in his father's whisky. In a country where advertising is king, Akuto, instead, focused on the best marketing of all—damn fine whisky.

After getting a whisky-storing license in 2008, Akuto purchased the precious casks from Sasanokawa, containing whisky that remained from the Hanyu Distillery. That stock produced some of the most valuable Japanese whiskies ever released. In 2015, a set of 54 Hanyu whiskies Akuto selected and bottled as individual playing cards sold for around US$490,000 at auction in Hong Kong, one of the largest sums ever paid for a Japanese whisky lot.

Akuto calls the price "crazy." Just think if Toa Shuzo's new owner had just sat on that Hanyu whisky!

After the worldwide acclaim, Toa Shuzo's new owner now seems interested in whisky, releasing its Golden Horse blends made from imported Scottish malt. Little remains of the original Hanyu Distillery. One of the stills, the wash still, sits in front of the Venture Whisky Distillery as a reminder of the heritage this young maker has. The other one, the spirit still, went to Chichibu Kikusui Shuzo, the sake and drinks maker run by his relatives. There it was repurposed as a shochu still and was distilling as late as 2014.

The Birth of Venture Whisky

As rural as Venture Whisky's distillery location is, it's still located in a corporate office park. Right across the road is a data security company, which is fitting considering the venture nature of this distillery.

"When I first talked about setting up a distillery, bartenders were encouraging," Akuto says. "They thought it would be interesting if there were more Japanese whisky distilleries than just the big ones." Bankers were less so, wondering why anyone would want to make a distillery in Japan with such sagging whisky sales. Akuto pointed out that things might be bad domestically but singles malt sales were up internationally and he wanted to make a whisky that was sold worldwide.

With venture funding secured, a Shinto purification ritual, common whenever most buildings in Japan are built, was held in July 2007 at the distillery's ground-breaking ceremony. By year's end, construction was

Far left Unlike most other Japanese distilleries, Venture Whisky's kiln isn't for the sake of appearances but can be used to dry malted barley.
Left To make the barley germinate, it's necessary to maintain a temperature of 13–16 °C (55–60 °F) during the floor malting.
Center far left Sprouts stick out of floor-malted Japanese barley.
Left To malt the barley, a malster must continuously turn over the malt by hand. Repetitive strain injuries have traditionally been common, so these days large commercial malt makers turn the malt in enormous rotating drums.
Below left Chichibu's mash tun is small enough that the sugary wort is stirred by hand instead of by machine. Notice that the mash tun's lid is covered with kakishibu (for more on this, see page 41).

completed. "At that time I was asked, 'Are you happy?' It was less that I was happy and more that things had gotten very real. It was less a happy feeling but more of an awareness that this would not be easy." Three years later, Chichibu had its first whisky.

"Most of the three-year-old Scotch whiskies I've had always felt too young, like they needed more maturation," Akuto says, "but when I tried our first whisky, which was only three years old, I thought this is different and that people would enjoy drinking it." The Chichibu Distillery released Ichiro's Malt Chichibu The First, and all 7,400 bottles sold out in one day. Venture Whisky was off and running.

The Chichibu Way

Unlike most other Japanese distilleries, the Chichibu Distillery's pagoda isn't only for looks. It's for a fully functional kiln to dry malted barley. On the other side of the distillery is a malting floor where distillery workers malt a small percentage of Japanese barley to go in

their whiskies. "We should've put the floor closer to the kiln because it's a bit of a pain in the butt to transport the malted barley across the distillery," says brand manager Yumi Yoshikawa. Malting barley is hard, time-consuming work because the traditional way of doing it is often the hardest way. Most of the whisky, however, is made from imported malted barley.

"This isn't a craft distillery," Yoshikawa is quick to point out. "It's a traditional one. The idea behind Chichibu is 'Back to traditional.'" The distinction might be craft and traditional might be one of nuance, but even for such a young distillery there's a sense of heritage and lineage. Akuto takes his distillery staff on regular trips to Scotland where they can get experience working in places like the Springbank Distillery in Campbeltown.

Inside the distillery, Taro Okuyama checks his watch as the milled barley steeps in hot water. Covering the tank is a wooden lid that's been varnished

Above This is the only distillery using mizunara washbacks for fermentation.
Above right The bubbly wash or brewer's beer Chichibu ferments has an elegant sake-like aroma.
Left Glasses filled with samples are lined up on the spirit safe as the stillman looks for the distillate's heart.
Below At Chichibu, distillers keep track of the time and temperature to track the distillation run. They also rely on taste and smell when making the cut.

Right The human nose is one of the most powerful instruments to check the distillate run. The early part of the distillation has too many volatile compounds to make suitable whisky. The distillation's heart is aged in wood, while the rest of the run is funnelled back for reuse in future distillations.

with *kakishibu*, the juice from persimmon tannins, turning it a brownish orange hue. This is a common strategy at sake breweries to waterproof the wood. Okuyama is handling the mashing today. He checks his watch once more time and gets a wooden paddle. At 23, he's young, but most everyone here at Chichibu Distillery is, with an average age of 30. Most distilleries don't do this by hand, instead using a mechanized contraption, but Chichibu can because the tank is so small. Okuyama stirs gently, holding the middle of the bamboo paddle's shaft between his fingers, but keeping it steady with his right hand.

A soft, elegant aroma fills the air. It's subtle, carbonated and reminiscent of the scent found at sake breweries. The *mizunara* washbacks, unique in whisky production, have been filled, and climbing up a ladder and taking a peek in, the top is white and fluffy. A blade spins around the top, preventing the bubbles from overflowing. It's the first day of fermentation. On the second day, the scent changes to apples, pineapples and papayas. By the third day, it's yogurt and melons.

On the other side of the fermentation tanks sit two squat onion-shaped pot stills. Their doors proudly read "Scotland." Okuyama, now working as the stillman, is looking closely at a thermometer in the spirit safe to see when he has to make the cut. Next to him stands Akuto as three men, who appear to be in their twenties, look on. Decked out in *sagyofuku*, or Japanese work clothes often seen at factories, they've come from Sasanokawa Shuzo, the drinks maker who helped Akuto save Hanyu's malt whisky.

"We've been distilling whisky but hope to learn how to improve what we're producing," says one of the trio. They're scribbling copious notes as the stillman opens the spirit safe, takes a sample in a glass and places it on a makeshift table, writing the exact time the sample was taken in marker on the glass's base. Okuyama is looking for the heart so he can cut it for new whisky. At 9.16 am, the spirit is pleasant but there are still some undesirable notes. At 9.17 am it's better, and then, at 9.18 am he locates the heart and Akuto gives the okay. The stillman makes the cut and switches the flow of the whisky. This is the spirit that will go into barrels and become Ichiro's Malt. The three visitors in workman's clothes take notes and compare the head and heart samples for themselves.

Behind the stills, off to the side is a *kamidana*, a small Shinto shrine on the wall. It hangs high up because kamidana aren't supposed to be at eye level. Inside the shrine, there's a *shimenawa*, a Shinto rope used to mark off a holy area, and a glass filled with a clear liquid. It's an offering to the *kami*, or deity. "It's actually water," Yoshikawa says. "Don't want the kami to drink too much." Kamidana like this are not an uncommon sight in sake breweries, creating a small space for worship and to make offerings. "This is less to ensure good whisky," Yoshikawa says,

"than to protect the distillery and ensure the workers' safety."

Top This sticker from Chichibu Shrine shows a vehicle has been blessed for "traffic safety." In this case, it was on a distillery forklift.

Above left Besides making casks, cooper Kenta Nagae stacks and moves casks in Chichibu's warehouses.

Left Mizunara logs from Hokkaido air-dry out front before they're ready for splitting. In the background are Venture Whisky's newest maturation warehouses. They are dark-colored to draw heat and speed up the aging process.

Venture Whisky's Warehouses

Inside, it's cool and pleasant. The scent of oak and caramel fills the air. Like all the warehouses at Chichibu, this is dunnage style, with earth floors and casks stacked three and four high. Over half of the casks are bourbon barrels as well as other cask like puncheon, port pipe, hogsheads and sherry butts together with rum, cognac and wine casks—you name it. There are also Chichibu originals. "This is what we call a *chibidaru*, which we use to age whisky faster," says Kenta Nagae, the cooper, pointing to a small cask. "That's why we put them up on the fourth level so they mature more quickly." "Chibidaru" literally means

"little cask," and at around 130 liters (34 gallons) the size of these custom creations is closest to a quarter cask.

The warehouse pops and creaks as the weather warms up. Nagae begins moving out several casks, requiring him to move all the surrounding casks just to get to them. It's laborious and difficult, especially because he's doing it solo, rolling each 250-kg (550-pound) cask along the second tier planks to a Toyota forklift, on the back of which is a sticker denoting that a Shinto priest has blessed the vehicle for safety. Getting the casks down is a calculated, physically demanding task. Nagae takes his time, carefully moving each cask on the palette, rocking it gently onto

Another Round at One Shot Bar Keith

"For me, everything changed in 2006," says Bar Keith's Teruhiko Yamamoto. "I discovered that Japanese whisky would be my life's work." His Osaka bar had been serving up Scotch and bourbon, but increasingly Yamamoto began to refocus. By 2012 the bar began serving a white label Chichibu blend as its house whisky. Today, the bar is one of a few Japanese whisky specialty bars in the country. Yes, Japan is home to world whisky bars with impressive Japanese collections as well as Nikka bars and Suntory bars specializing in each maker, but there are only a handful that concentrate completely on Japanese whisky.

"Chichibu, in particular, has made a huge impact on me," Yamamoto says. "As a bartender I was impressed that Ichiro-san took his whisky to countless bars when he was just getting starting to build relationships, and that not only was he able to set up a distillery he then made wonderful whisky. As a Japanese, that makes me proud."

Bar Keith's walls are still covered with Jack Daniels and Ardbeg signs and there are a few stray Johnnie Walker bottles from the old days. There are Venture Whisky posters mixed in here and there, while the shelves are nearly exclusively lined with Japanese whisky. In recent years, the number of tourists coming into the bar, eager to drink local stuff, has spiked. "The population in Japan is decreasing, so without a doubt the future of Japanese whisky lies outside our borders," he says.

Japan's whisky tradition isn't yet a hundred years old and much of its whisky story is still unwritten. "I always tell people not to worry about not being able to drink certain older whiskies that are no longer available, like Karuizawa or Hanyu, because there's always great whisky around the corner," pointing out that Chichibu gets better and better, and there are more and more new distilleries. "Scotch whisky has a long tradition, but right now it feels like Japanese whisky is entering a brand new chapter," he says. "We're seeing whisky history right before our eyes."

a wood slab, moving it down to the ground, kicking out the slab and rolling the cask down the warehouse.

The Coopers of Chichibu

"I'm one of the older ones here," the 36-year-old Nagae says. For 12 years he worked as a cooper for the Kagoshima shochu distillery Satsuma Shuzo, but when he heard about the Chichibu Distillery he packed his bags and showed up unannounced on the doorstep, looking for work. "At the shochu distillery, I only remade barrels and had heard that they had wanted to make new casks here," Nagae says. "I thought if I could get a job here, I could expand my cooper skills."

Nagae comes from a proud tradition of Japan's greatest Western-style coopers. While handling casks for Satsuma Shuzo, Nagae's master was Hirotsugu Hayasaka, who had previously worked for decades as a cooper at Nikka. His master was Ryoichi Sasaki, who was an apprentice under Yoshiro Komatsuzaki, the cask

Above left These mizunara logs will be turned into some of the most desirable and difficult casks in the whisky business.
Above Splitting *mizunara* with an axe keeps the grain intact and makes the casks less leak-prone.

maker hand-picked by Masataka Taketsuru when he founded Nikka. Through the apprenticeships, there is a direct line from Nikka's first legendary cask maker to right here in Chichibu.

The cooperage is a hanger down the road from the main distillery buildings, next to a row of new maturation warehouses, one of which is painted black. "That's to speed up the aging process," Nagae says. Inside the cooperage it smells woody, burnt and metallic. Old cask-making machines

were purchased from Mitsuo Saito, the president and master cooper at Maru S ("Circle S", with the letter referring to "Saito"), the cooperage that refurbished casks for the Hanyu Distillery.

"When I moved to Hanyu in the late 1960s I didn't know there was a distillery there," says Saito, who sold his excellent casks to Nikka as well as to wine and shochu makers. When he and his wife, a Hanyu native, moved to her hometown, Saito opened a brand-new cooperage on a big stretch of land. "I was driving down the road when I saw these buildings with casks stacked out front," says Saito, "and that's when I learned they made whisky in Hanyu." According to him, he doesn't recall making new casks for Hanyu but says he mostly refurbished bourbon barrels as well as some sherry casks. Now in his early nineties, Saito hung up his tools and calls Tokyo home, but his old equipment, some of which he designed and had built, is still being used at Chichibu. That same spirit of innovation lives on at Venture Whisky today, with the distillery coming up with new cask-making machines and techniques to split wood better and craft non-leaky mizunara casks.

Nagae hammers the hoop in place on an older cask. Clank, clank, clank echoes throughout the warehouse. It's rare for large whisky makers to make

Above While the old Hanyu Distillery's wash still now sits in front of the Chichibu Distillery, the spirit still (pictured) found a second life in shochu distillation.

Below The mizunara trees planted next to Venture Whisky's office won't be cask-ready for another 150 years. Even then, because of Chichibu's temperature, the grain might not be tight enough for quality casks. That's not the point. These trees represent the big dreams of a small distillery.

their casks on-site and even rarer for them to make their casks directly from logs. At Ariake Barrel, for example, Japanese oak arrives pre-cut on palettes direct from Hokkaido, ready to be turned into casks. At Chichibu they're doing it on-site. In front of the cooperage sits a row of mizunara logs imported from Hokkaido. Nagae picks one up and carries it into the cooperage. He stands the log under a hoop machine that's been modified with an axe head into a wood-splitting machine. The axe splits the mizunara along the grain, and the halves are then split into even smaller pieces. Then he cuts them into even smaller, more workable wood, which he will make into staves for precious mizunara casks. All of this is done along the grain to make notoriously leaky mizunara less so.

Those freshly cut wood staves, however, aren't ready to be made into casks. First, they need to be air-dried outside to reduce the moisture in the wood. At Chichibu, the mizunara staves are left to dry for three years,

but even after that period the wood moisture is 18 percent. The drying, however, is finished in a kiln to get the staves down to the desired 15 percent moisture, a target that means the wood is still workable but won't shrink any further. Open-air drying is considered preferable, slowly softening undesirable flavors in the staves, but because it takes so long to get the mizunara ready for casks Chichibu has been running kiln-drying tests.

In the world of whisky, this new wood is just beginning its life. "Long after I'm dead, these casks will still be around," Nagae says, looking at his handiwork. "They can be used 50–80 years in the future. I do think about that while I'm making them."

The Next Generation of Japanese Whisky Makers

After years of stagnation, the Japanese whisky business is growing. "Yes, there is a Japanese whisky boom," Akuto says, taking a sip of coffee in Chichibu's reception area. "But more than that I think people are finally reappraising Japanese whisky."

New distilleries are opening up across Japan and a new generation is learning the craft. "Every year, young people have come here saying that they want to make whisky," Akuto says. Not all of them can be hired, obviously, but young Japanese have never been keener on whisky than now.

Unlike larger whisky makers, who might

place new hires in an office, those who do get jobs at Venture Whisky are put on the distillery floor and given the chance to learn how to make whisky. Heck, even people from other distilleries are given that chance, as evident by the trio from Sasanokawa, who were following Chichibu staff around, watching them work and taking notes so they can improve their own process.

"I remember when I was at Suntory and looking at the official internal corporate history book, there was nothing about Taketsuru," he says. Akuto doesn't want the Japanese whisky industry to be built around the fierce rivalries of the past, with each company seeming to want to obliterate the competition, but rather hopes distilleries can work together like in Scotland.

"When a new distillery opens in Japan, that's good for the Japanese whisky business," he says. "It means that people are interested in Japanese whisky. If more distilleries open, that means people have a bigger selection of whisky. I want other small distilleries to make a good product. It'll benefit us all."

TASTING NOTES FOR 15 VENTURE WHISKIES

By Yuji Kawasaki

It's said that Chichibu whiskies don't yet have their own distillery character, which isn't quite true. The distillery is known for its wide range, for making exceedingly good whisky and for not being afraid to experiment and try new things. Those qualities mark a Chichibu whisky.

Asta Morris Chichibu Ichiro's Malt 5 Years Old (2010–2016) 78/100

Here we have a Chichibu bottling for Belgium's Asta Morris. It has a sweet bouquet that's straightforward but not complex, with a bit of dark chocolate on arrival. Regal stuff. It would make for a nice weekend dram, sitting around a wooden table at the seashore, tapping your fingers and with a large-breed dog nearby.

Ichiro's Malt and Grain 85/100

The label says this is a "worldwide blend." Price-wise Ichiro's Malt and Grain is Venture Whisky's entry-level drink and it's quite good. Morning beach air and the taste of mangoes, strawberries and bananas for a sweet, sleepy finish.

Ichiro's Malt and Grain Premium 87/100

The more expensive black label version of Venture Whisky's "worldwide blend," first released back in 2012. The warm smell of strawberry jam being made in a saucepan on the stove, followed by distinct apple notes. This blend slowly heats up, like a refreshing, early summer day with fresh linen and rounds of golf. It creates a hankering for savory meat, like roast beef, to be enjoyed with an elegant sunset.

Ichiro's Malt Chichibu Chibidaru 86/100

"Chibidaru" literally means "little cask" and the term refers to Chichibu's version of a quarter cask. Nosing the glass there are honey and strawberries followed by acidic smoke. What else? Figs, walnuts and almonds, but as though they were all lined up on a wooden table. On arrival, sharp notes develop into delightfully crisp spices. Not a punchy or a grandiose whisky but, rather, one with depth.

Ichiro's Malt Chichibu for HBA 82/100

Distilled in 2010 and bottled in 2016, this exclusive limited release (only 328 bottles!) was made for the Hotel Barmen's Association, Japan. There are bananas, muscat grapes, mangos, even risotto. The strong alcohol notes teeter, just barely balanced. Bottled at 59.5 percent, it's the alcohol that first jumps out. The whisky then gradually quiets down. The sprightly elements are refined, while the refined elements are too lively. It's interesting because this

Asta Morris Chichibu Ichiro's Malt 5 Years Old

Ichiro's Malt and Grain

whisky feels finished yet still like a work in progress. Here's a chance to savor that fluid, in-between experience.

Ichiro's Malt Chichibu Newborn Bourbon Barrel 4 Months **87/100**

A very, very young expression from 2008, the early days of Venture Whisky. It's only spent four months in a bourbon barrel and couldn't yet be called "whisky" for yet another 32 months. That said, this super limited bottling provides a fascinating time capsule of Chichibu's early distillate. First impression is the unassuming sweetness of *mizuame* (literally "water candy"), a clear sticky sweetener made by turning starches into sugars. It's lucid, reminiscent of a starry night. Lurking behind blunt *umami* flavors are blooming flowers. The finish is hot and heavy.

Ichiro's Malt Chichibu Newborn New Hogshead 6 Months Old **84/100**

Distilled in 2008, this was aged for only six months in a new hogshead cask made from American white oak. While it wouldn't yet classify as whisky, this new spirit was bottled to show how the distillery was progressing towards its first three-year-old whiskies. Like furniture specially made to a master carpenter's exact specifications, you can really feel the work that's gone into this spirit. But it doesn't come in shouting and tooting its own horn. Instead, this Chichibu just opens up softly, only wanting you to savor the experience. And just like a new table, over time, it seems like this new-make will develop even more texture. But for now it's still freshly put together and a way to taste Venture Whisky's craftsmanship.

Ichiro's Malt Chichibu Chibidaru

Ichiro's Malt Chichibu Port Pipe

Ichiro's Malt Chichibu Port Pipe **80/100**

If you tilt the glass and draw your nose near, you're first hit with the scents of high-proof brandy and acidic port wine. That's followed by ginger and spicy cask notes. Going deeper into this whisky reveals unripe persimmons and rum raisins in fresh cream. Bottled at cask strength of 54.5 percent abv, the strong alcohol comes in hot, but within that there are crushed raisins and lemon. The cask flavors do not go unnoticed, and this whisky insists on pushing spices through to the point of risking its balance. It seems like the whole thing is on the verge of collapse. If would be more enjoyable if those spices had the day off.

Ichiro's Malt Chichibu Whisky Festival 2017 **89/100**

Every February Venture Whisky oversees a festival at Chichibu Shrine, and every year more and more people attend. In 2017, over 3,000 people showed up! For the festival, Venture Whisky does an extremely limited bottling of 293, with a raffle for the chance to buy this desirable whisky.

This 2017 bottling is six years old and matured in a Fino sherry hogshead cask. The result is a top aroma that is lucidly deep and elegant. The scents are arranged systematically, like a piano's black and white keys. But what's that in the background? An earthy field in spring. On the palette spicy notes provide solos, with an unassuming orchestra following the melody. Light and airy but profound.

Ichiro's Malt Chichibu X Kusuda Bottled in 2015 **65/100**

A made-in-Japan whisky matched with a made-in-New-Zealand wine. "Ichiro," of course, refers to Chichibu Distillery founder Ichiro Akuto. "Kusuda" is Hiroyuki Kusuda, a law grad who moved to New Zealand to set up his own vineyard, only to become one of that country's rising wine makers. So, maturing Ichiro's excellent whisky in a cask that held Kusuda's wonderful wine is an automatic win, right? This time around, not quite. This whisky feels a bit overworked. There's the fragrance of dark and yellow orchids along with strong wine notes. But on the palate the whisky doesn't settle down and keeps running ahead at full speed until it's exhausted and you are, too.

Ichiro's Malt Chichibu Zoetrope Banzai Across the 8th Anniversary
89/100

A special bottling for Tokyo whisky bar Zoetrope to celebrate its 8th anniversary, so you won't find it in the shops. Distilled in 2009 and aged in a bourbon barrel, the first thing that hits are dry raisins followed by rather astringent notes. This whisky packs a big, crisp punch. Even though it has the same sweetness you'd find in brandy, it's very aggressive! Which is why this bottling is interesting. It's rebellious but still grown up.

Ichiro's Malt Double Distilleries
88/100

A blend of whiskies from the mothballed Hanyu Distillery, which Venture Whisky founder Ichiro Akuto's father owned, and the Chichibu Distillery. The dominant aromas here evoke camping during fall, sweeping of leaves, cool skies, warm jackets, sweet pine cones and dried fig. Calm like early afternoon in the mountains, this is a surprisingly soft whisky, which really opens up in the palette. It has flavors you don't often taste in whiskies, and you could totally drink this at teatime with little cookies.

Ichiro's Malt Five of Spades **87/100**

This wasn't distilled at Chichibu but is one of the whiskies Ichiro Akuto saved after his family's business was taken over. The Five of Spades was distilled in 2000, the last year the Hanyu Distillery was in operation, but bottled

Ichiro's Malt Double Distilleries

Ichiro's Malt MWR

in 2008 at a whopping 60.5 percent abv, a strength you don't usually come across in Japan. Akuto released 54 different whiskies in this playing card series. So, how's the five of spades?

The aromas just float up and engulf your senses. It's as though you're returning to your family home in the Japanese countryside. There's a warm bushel of flowers and a slightly open wooden gate leading into a house with a dining table. On it there are grapes and pears waiting to be devoured. Tastewise, there's *karinto*, a crunchy snack covered with unrefined black sugar, smoke and burnt cereals. That's followed by black tea. The Five of Spades is full-bodied, and for only an eight-year-old whisky it seems surprisingly mellow at first but it's followed by a spicy finish.

Ichiro's Malt MWR **83/100**

"MWR" as in "Mizunara Wood Reserve." Initially, there's the delicious scent of cooked rice. But this isn't the aroma you get from an electric rice cooker but, rather, from rice boiled with fresh stream water in a kettle outdoors. There's also some chocolate in the background. Mizunara's particular bitterness is readily apparent in the flavor. It's not a deep, piercing bitterness but, rather, it lingers gracefully in the mouth, much like the nuanced taste found in the charred salted skin of grilled freshwater fish. The bitter flavor's unique harmony is truly lovely.

Ichiro's Malt Two of Clubs **95/100**

The thing about a well-tailored silk shirt is that even though it's neat and orderly you can still feel the creator's burning passion. It's a gentle fastidiousness. That describes this Ichiro bottling of a Hanyu whisky. The nose is utterly enchanting. It passes through like an arm going into a sleeve until it's one with you in a relaxing and natural way. The aromas are so complex that it seems as though nearly anything can be interpreted in them. As with clothing, what you bring to this whisky is just as important as what it brings to you. The finish, though, is unexpectedly robust, like the rugged hands of an artisan. Exceptional stuff.

Afterword

The Future of Japanese Whisky

Purple wild flowers surround a worn dirt path that leads to one of Japan's newest whisky makers, the Akkeshi Distillery. It's one of several that entered production between 2016 and 2018. Located in a Hokkaido fishing village, it isn't Japan's northernmost distillery—Yoichi still claims that honor—but it is the easternmost. The port fills the nostrils with sea salt and ocean air, and the distillery is a short drive up a bluff overlooking the bay.

Akkeshi's landscape, with its marshes and hills, might remind some of Scotland. If it doesn't, perhaps the Scottish flag flying next to the Japanese one in front of the distillery's office might do the trick! "Compared to Scotland, the temperature differences between hot and cold at Akkeshi are drastic," says Keiichi Toita, president of Kenten Co. Ltd, a food products company that set up this distillery. During winter, the temperature can drop to -20 °C (-4 °F) with an average temp of -5 °C (23 °F). Summer doesn't see the heat creep over 25 °C (77 °F). These extreme temperature variations, Toita believes, make a "unique aging environment" and will result in distinct Akkeshi's whiskies.

Toita first got the idea of making whisky back in 2010. "We're originally in the food business and a few years ago we started exporting Japanese whisky," says Toita. "But when the Japanese whisky boom exploded, it became hard to obtain stock so that's when we set our sights on making our own whisky." It wasn't until 2013 that the first maturation tests began, with spirit distilled in Saitama filling four casks (three virgin white oak casks and one sherry cask) and spirit distilled by Eigashima Shuzo filling four more (one ex-brandy cask, one sherry cask and two virgin white oak casks). In the fall of 2016, once construction was completed, Akkeshi began distilling its own spirit.

What's also distinct is that Akkeshi's distillery house style will be heavily peated, with limited unpeated distillation runs. This production method is the opposite of many Japanese distilleries, which use unpeated malt whisky as their base line, with sporadic peated distillations.

Going Local

"We definitely don't lack local peat," says Toita. "We're currently researching the differences between Hokkaido peat and Scottish peat," says Toita. "Since the vegetation isn't the same, we do believe there will be a considerable difference in flavor." In decades past, when Nikka still used Japanese barley, it dried the malt with Hokkaido peat, the availability of which was one reason why Masataka Taketsuru picked the island for his distillery.

Akkeshi first test-aged whiskies from other distilleries. Eigashima Distillery refers to Eigashima Shuzo's White Oak Distillery, while "Araside" is a branding name for a famous Saitama-based whisky maker.

The hope is to eventually use local peat and a percentage of Japanese barley in the Akkeshi whiskies. "But we're a few years from that," says Toita. As the company begins distillation, it's importing Scottish barley. Akkeshi might be starting with Scottish barley but it's not the only new distillery interested in a domestic crop.

Following in the footsteps of the Chichibu Distillery, expect an increasing number of Japanese distilleries to use a percentage of or experiment with local peat and barley. Going fully local for all releases will be difficult. Due to cost and production pipelines, imported grain will continue to dominate at large and small makers alike.

The Shizuoka Distillery, which was also established in 2016, has been using a relatively new type of high-quality Japanese barley called Sachiho Golden, developed to compete with imported barley and often used in Japanese pilsner beers. "In the first year, the plan is to use 45 tons of domestic barley," says the distillery's founder Taiko Nakamura. "While this isn't yet fixed, I think domestic barley will be about 20–30 percent of all that we use." Nearby farmers are now growing barley for whisky production.

Nakamura's company Gaiaflow was originally a whisky importer and bottler but his dream was always to make his own whisky. The distillery—done in a modern Japanese style—looks distinct as most others look to Scottish distilleries for inspiration. "I wanted the Shizuoka Distillery to be immediately recognizable from the outside, so that's why I chose a modern Japanese architectural style."

Inside is also unique. The wash still is fired by burning wood, something no other distillery in Japan does. Four of Gaiaflow's fermentation tanks are made of Oregon pine, which is common, but it also has a fifth made from local Japanese cedar, with more

Mist covers a mountain behind Gaiaflow's Shizuoka Distillery. When it was first completed, the building's face read "Gaiaflow" but it now reads "The Shizuoka Distillery."

planned for future installment. While Japanese cedar has a fresh sharpness, according to Gaiaflow the Japanese cedar fermentation tank is producing a fruity spirit. Initially, Shizuoka is using a dry distiller's yeast but Nakamura is looking at also using ale yeast, adding even more flavors and aromas. As the distillery finds its footing, maturation is first-fill bourbon barrels, but Nakamura is interested in other options— sherry casks, smaller casks, new casks, wine casks and more.

Nakamura shelled out 5.05 million yen (US$45,000) at auction for the legendary Karuizawa Distillery's remaining equipment. "Included in this were four pot stills, but the copper was so worn in places there were holes," he says. "Salvaging parts from all four, we were able to assemble one complete still." Nakamura had a new steam coil added, and Karuizawa now lives on as a wash still in Shizuoka, joining two of the distillery's newly installed Forsyths stills from Scotland. Karuizawa's Porteus mill was in far better shape and continues to grind grain at the Shizuoka Distillery.

Similarly, the Kiuchi Brewery is also going local, aiming to distil distinctively Japanese whisky. Founded in 1823, Kiuchi Brewery makes sake, wine and shochu, but is perhaps best known for its Hitachino Nest Beer— aka that excellent Japanese craft beer with the owl logo. Located in Ibaraki Prefecture, the brewery installed a hybrid still in 2016 to begin test distilling whisky at the brewery. Kiuchi Brewery plans to make its new Nukuda Distillery operational in March 2018 with imported Scottish stills, using their beer know-how to make excellent Japanese stuff.

"We're going to put out a 100 percent domestic release," says Kiuchi Brewery's director Toshiyuki Kiuchi, the eighth generation to run the family business. The brewery is using domestic barley Asuka Golden and Kaneko Golden, the last of which is a historically important variety, having both been malted in the country by Japanese beer maltsters. Kaneko Golden is the first beer barley variety cultivated in Japan and was created in 1900 when a farmer named Ushigoro Kaneko cross-pollinated American barley variety Golden Melon with a Japanese barley variety for noodles called Shikoku to make Kaneko Golden.

"In Ibaraki Prefecture, we had the largest beer barley cultivation in Japan until we joined GATT," says Kiuchi. In 1955, Japan signed onto the General Agreement on Tariffs and Trade, and according to Kiuchi, barley production in Ibaraki nearly fell to zero. "It resulted in so much abandoned farmland," he says. "In order to help rectify this, around 10 years ago, we began cultivating Kaneko Golden for one of our beers to help revive local barley production." The brewery procured 16 seeds from the country's Department of Agricultural History and spent five years getting the long-lost barley variety to grow. Now Kiuchi wants to turn the revived crop into spirit at its newly erected distillery, where the focus is on crafting unique Japanese whisky by using its drink making expertise and tapping its 10 or so yeast varieties that include ale and lager yeasts used in its award-winning beers. The pot stills, however, are Scottish—a fitting nod to Japan's whisky heritage.

Besides local barley and peat, Japanese *mizunara* will continue to help define Japanese whisky, as will more and more local woods, such as sakura and Japanese cedar, among others. Since the country does not have laws requiring whisky to be aged in oak, and with Ariake Barrel, a major supplier to small and medium-sized makers, introducing different woods for maturation, expect more whisky makers to experiment as a way to differentiate themselves and create new expressions. Kiuchi Brewery, for example, has been running maturation tests with sakura cask lids for future releases.

Local grain whisky production might prove more difficult. While Nikka and Suntory have their own integrated production process, domestic grain whisky production has been out of reach for most small to medium Japanese makers, meaning they have to rely on imported spirit. However, Mars Hombo has began procuring Japanese-made grain whisky for its blends, and the new Akkeshi Distillery hopes to one day set up its own grain distillery instead of relying on imports. Shochu makers with column stills also might be a future source for domestic grain whisky for blends.

The Emergence of New and Old Makers

Akkeshi, Shizuoka and Nukuda aren't the only new kids on the block. Okayama-based Miyashita Shuzo, a well-known sake brewer and drinks maker, has also started distilling spirit, and there are bound to be more. But Japanese whisky is experiencing more than a boom. For some, this is a rebirth. Besides brand-new makers, previously neglected or mothballed distilleries are being resurrected.

Drinks maker Sasanokawa Shuzo, which first got its whisky-making license in 1946, installed new stills

Top The date on the cask refers to when the Nukuda Distillery spirit was put in wood.
Above The Nukuda Distillery's original hybrid still. Kiuchi Brewery started distilling with this to find its footing before moving on to large Scottish-made pot stills.

in 2015. Sasanokawa's budget-priced Cherry brand whisky was a smash hit during the 1980s. But after the Japanese whisky business went south, it stopped distilling whisky and instead focused on shochu and sake, only purchasing whisky spirit from other distilleries to blend and sell. It was Sasanokawa that helped Chichibu's Ichiro Akuto save 400 casks of Hanyu whisky, and Akuto returned the favor by offering his know-how to Sasanokawa's young distillery workers so they can produce a better whisky.

Wakatsuru Shuzo is another maker that's revamping production. Originally a sake brewery established in 1862, it got a whisky license in 1952. The drinks maker raised over 38 million yen (US$335,000) in 2016 via online crowd-funding to help cover renovation of its Saburomaru Distillery, which had fallen into disrepair.

Not all the new distilleries need extensive construction work, or even that much space. A case in point is the Naga-hama Distillery. Located in northern Shiga Prefecture, it's the smallest whisky distillery in Japan with a 1,000-liter (264-gallon) wash still and a 500-liter (132-gallon) spirit still. The Portuguese-made copper alembic stills are shoehorned behind the restaurant's bar for all the patrons to see. Whisky distillation began in late 2016 but the restaurant and in-house craft beer brewery were established in 1996. Ex-bourbon casks are stacked at the end of the bar, and two mizunara casks rest near the wall. The air-conditioned restaurant inside might not be an ideal maturation environment. Nagahama Distillery is talking with the city of Nagahama about converting an abandoned tunnel into a whisky maturation warehouse.

"I think whisky making has been relatively smooth for us because we have beer expertise," says Nagahama's 32-year-old production chief Futoshi Okumura. He got his start at the restaurant waiting tables before moving up to beer brewery. He's one of four employees now making both beer and whisky. It's a small operation, and Okumura adds that restaurant staff help with the bottling when not waiting tables.

For its whisky, Nagahama uses both imported non-peated Germany malted barley and peated Scottish malt as well as industrial distiller's yeast. "In the future, after we have more experience, we'd like to use our beer yeasts in our whisky making," says Okumura.

While it waits for its first whisky to hit the three-year mark, the Nagahama Distillery began bottling and selling its new-make spirit, like some distilleries abroad do, but with a Japanese twist. Nagahama's restaurant serves up new-make highballs with *yuzu* citrus. The raw, unaged spirit has fruity menthol notes, and the distillery has been tweaking parts of its process, such as varying the fermentation temperature. Considering how several

hundred years ago whisky wasn't aged, bottling and selling unaged spirit isn't just a good business idea but a nod to the past.

What's Next for Japanese Whisky?

Unlike Scotch whisky, Japanese whisky isn't bound by tradition or rules but, rather, to convention. It has followed Scotch whisky-making conventions but integrated its own customs and culture into the process. The country's whisky will continue to evolve with new generations of whisky makers. Traditions are handed down but conventions can and do change.

Long-standing truths about Japanese whisky, such the country's

Below left Since helping to save the Hanyu casks, Sasanokawa Shuzo launched its new Asaka Distillery in 2016.

Right The Nagahama Distillery puts the micro in micro distillery. It's the only distillery in Japan you can literally sit right next to, eat roast beef or fish and chips, and drink newly distilled unaged spirit served highball style with a twist of citrus. In the background on the second floor are the fermentation tanks, which are used for whisky and beer production.

Below The Nagahama Distillery uses copper Portuguese-made Hoga alembic stills, which are ideal for tiny distilleries.

Below right Since the distillery is so small, there isn't enough space for dedicated spirit receiver tanks when making the cut during a distillation run. Instead, small plastic containers are used.

whisky makers don't trade casks, are bound to do just that. Small and medium-sized makers are expressing interest in working together. At Akkeshi, for example, Keiichi Toita says the distillery is "definitely" interested in swapping stock with other makers—ditto for Eigashima Shuzo and Venture Whisky. No doubt Japan's long tradition of not swapping

whiskies will eventually end, at least among smaller distilleries.

These new players are already showing a willingness to experiment, further redefining what Japanese whisky is. Will there be false starts and failures? Probably. But with experience they'll improve, just like Japan's first whisky makers did.

"The rise of new distillers will help

revitalize the business," says Shizuoka Distillery's Taiko Nakamura. This does not mean corporate giants won't innovate and make brilliant stuff. They will. Suntory and Nikka will continue playing a decisive and important role as upstarts bring fresh ideas. If you think Japanese whisky is good now, just wait another 10 or 15 years. It'll be even better.

Published by Tuttle Publishing, an imprint of Periplus Editions (HK) Ltd

www.tuttlepublishing.com

Copyright © 2018 Periplus Editions (HK) Ltd

Library of Congress Cataloging-in-Publication Data

Names: Ashcraft, Brian, author. | Bryson, Lew, writer of foreword. | Kawasaki, Yuji.
Title: Japanese whisky : The Ultimate Guide to the World's Most Desirable Spirit with Tasting Notes from Japan's Leading Whisky Blogger
  Brian Ashcraft ; with Idzuhiko Ueda and Yuji Kawasaki.
Description: Tokyo ; Rutland, Vermont : Tuttle Publishing, 2018.
Identifiers: LCCN 2017047168 | ISBN 9784805314098 (hardback)
Subjects: LCSH: Whiskey--Japan. | Whiskey industry--Japan. | BISAC: COOKING / Beverages / Wine & Spirits. | TRAVEL / Asia / Japan. | HISTORY / Asia / Japan.
Classification: LCC TP605 .A84 2018 | DDC 663/.52--dc23 LC record available at https://lccn.loc.gov/2017047168

ISBN: 978-4-8053-1409-8

Distributed by

North America, Latin America & Europe
Tuttle Publishing
364 Innovation Drive, North Clarendon, VT 05759-9436 U.S.A.
Tel: 1 (802) 773-8930, Fax: 1 (802) 773-6993
info@tuttlepublishing.com, www.tuttlepublishing.com

Japan
Tuttle Publishing
Yaekari Building 3rd Floor, 5-4-12 Osaki, Shinagawa-ku, Tokyo 141-0032
Tel: (81) 3 5437-0171, Fax: (81) 3 5437-0755
sales@tuttle.co.jp, www.tuttle.co.jp

Asia Pacific
Berkeley Books Pte. Ltd., 61 Tai Seng Avenue, #02-12
Singapore 534167, Tel: (65) 6280-1330, Fax: (65) 6280-6290
inquiries@periplus.com.sg, www.periplus.com

20 19 18   10 9 8 7 6 5 4 3 2

Printed in China   1807CM

About Tuttle "Books to Span the East and West"

Our core mission at Tuttle Publishing is to create books which bring people together one page at a time. Tuttle was founded in 1832 in the small New England town of Rutland, Vermont (USA). Our fundamental values remain as strong today as they were then—to publish best-in-class books informing the English-speaking world about the countries and peoples of Asia. The world has become a smaller place today and Asia's economic, cultural and political influence has expanded, yet the need for meaningful dialogue and information about this diverse region has never been greater. Since 1948, Tuttle has been a leader in publishing books on the cultures, arts, cuisines, languages and literatures of Asia. Our authors and photographers have won numerous awards and Tuttle has published thousands of books on subjects ranging from martial arts to paper crafts. We welcome you to explore the wealth of information available on Asia at **www.tuttlepublishing.com**.

Acknowledgments

This book would not have been possible without the insights and/or cooperation of many. Thank you to Takakeshi Abe, Kihei Abe IV, Yasutake Aikawa, Kazuhito Aizawa, Chieko Akuto, Ichiro Akuto, Yutaka Akuto, Takeshi Aoki, Hikoji Arai, Kunio Araya, Ryo Baba, Joan W. Bennett, Dave Broom, Lew Bryson, Chris Bunting, Olive Checkland, Shinichiro Chiba, Ryu Fujii, Kiyoshi Fujita, Fukuda Bar, Shinji Fukuyo, Kazuki Funao, Gotemba City Hall, Shunji Hatakeyama, Hirotsugu Hayasaka, Toshiyuki Hayashi, Tatsuya Hirayama, Futoshi Hirota, Osamu Igura, Kiyotaka Ishii, Akikazu Ito, Asami Iwamoto, Tira Izu, Michael Jackson, Hirofumi Kanda, Akiko Karino, Yuki Kashiwagi, Shinya Kawaguchi, Yuji Kawai, Toshikazu Kimura, Junji Kitadai, Yosuke Konishi, Azusa Konya at Bar Canmi, Yoshikazu Koyano, Tetsuji Kubota, Shizuko Kwata, Horst Luening, Charles MacLean, Jun Maeda, Michihiko Matsuba at Bar K, Michihiko Matsumoto, Shinji Matsushima, Christine McCafferty, Toshiyuki Mieda, Akayuki Mikami, Mio Museum, Ralfy Mitchell, Yukari Miyazaki, Miki Mizushima, Kayoko Murata, Kenta Nagae, Hironori Nagatomo, Kazuki Nakagawa, Haruko Nakahara, Yuji Nakamura, Daisaku Nakano, Hiroshi Nasu, Sasana Nemoto, The Nikka Bar, Nikka Bar Passina, Toshitaka Nishijima at Bar Amami, Koichi Nishikawa, Yashima Nishikita, Toshimasa Obitsu, Kiichiro Ochi, Tatsuya Oda, Takayoshi Odawara, Hisako Oiwake, Chie Okanobori, Futoshi Okumura, Kanae Omori, Makoto Ono, Osaka University Library, Hiroya Oshima, Osamu Oshita, Kazuhisa Owashi, Koji Oyanagi, Hasumi Ozawa, Clay Risen, Koshiro Sakoda, Tadashi Sakuma, Yoshihiro Samejima, Hidetada Sano, Tsuyoshi Sanno, Suekichi Sasaki, Yusuke Sasaki, Mikio Sato, Shigeo Sato, Tatsujiro Shimamiya, Shot Bar Zoetrope, Mark Skipworth, Hiroko Sonoi, Yoshimi Suzuki, Nanbu Takahara, Shoji Takahashi, Toshihiro Takai, Kazunori Takamine, Tomoe Takamizawa, Koki Takehira, Kazuya Tanabe, Shuji Tanaka, Takayuki Tanaka, Shigemi Tateyama, Katsuyuki Tatsusaki, Hiroshi Tsubouchi, Nobutoshi Tsuchiya, Yasuro Tsudome, Yasushi Tsuji, Saboro Terasawa, Hideaki Tomisako, Hiroaki Toumiya, Shiro Toyonaga, Katsunori Ueda, Urakawa Town Hall, Stefan Van Eycken, Masayuki Yabushita, Minoru Yamada, Kenzai Yamamoto, Minako Yamamoto, Teruhiko Yamamoto, Shogo Yamashita, Yoichi Town Hall, Yumi Yoshikawa, Mitsuko Yoshimura, Yumi Yoshino and Noboru Yorimoto.

Brian Ashcraft would like to thank Shoko, Ken, Louis, Ewan, his parents Ron and Joy, Kota, Kotaku (Stephen, Riley, Luke, Jason, Mike, Cecilia, Gita, Heather, Chris K., Chris P., Tim and Ethan), Gergo and Andras.

Izuhiko Ueda would like to thank Kyoko and Kota.

Yuji Kawasaki would like to thank Toshiharu Imaichi at Bar Imaichi, Kanae Kawasaki, Yu Kurahashi at Bar Tre, Ryo Matsumuro at Bar Flamingo and Makoto Nakafuda at Bar Nakafuda.

All photos by Izuhiko Ueda except for the following: Brian Ashcraft (pp. 41, 83, 98), P. S. Duval & Co, Heine, W. & Queen, J. F. (Library of Congress, p. 12), Great People of Kanazawa Memorial Museum (p. 24), Hiroshige (Library of Congress, p. 12), The Historiographical Institute, University of Tokyo (p. 12), Hokkaido University Library (p. 38), KPG_Payless (Shutterstock, p. 40), Yari Hotaka (color corrected, https://www.flickr.com/photos/miurasat/24823535911, p. 95), Kiuchi Brewery (pp. 57, 141), Mainichi Photobank (p. 17), Hiroshi Matsuda (p. 60), Hiromichi Murota (p. 109), Chris 73 (Thomas_Blake_Clover_Statue_Clover_Garden_Nagasaki.jpg, p. 21), Nikka (pp. 4, 10, 21, 22, 57, 86, 88, 91, 95, 98), Tatsujiro Shimamiya (courtesy of, pp. 90, 91), Hombo Shuzo (p. 107), Sasanokawa Shuzo (p. 57), Wakatsuru Shuzo (p. 57), Suntory (pp. 10, 11, 21, 23, 25, 42, 43, 50, 60), Taro Ueda (p. 47).